The Living Tao

Meditations on the *Tao Te Ching* to Empower Your Life

Stephen F. Kaufman, Hanshi 10th Dan

CHARLES E. TUTTLE CO., INC.
Boston ✦ Rutland, Vermont ✦ Tokyo

This book is dedicated to all children
and my special friend
Lianne Johnson
"Eleganza Preciosa"

Starflitter cosmos run run
Everywhere you go you have fun
Of confusions and errors there are none
Everything is understood and all one
And God simply is done

—Stephen F. Kaufman, from "Disavowals of Reason,"
January 20, 1982

First published in 1998 by Tuttle Publishing, an imprint of Periplus Editions (HK) Ltd.,
with editorial offices at 153 Milk Street, Boston, Massachusetts 02109.

Library of Congress Cataloging-in-Publication Data

Kaufman, Steve, 1939–
    The living Tao : meditations of the Tao te ching to empower your
life / Stephen Kaufman.
        p. cm.
    ISBN 0-8048-3143-2 (hc.)
    1. Lao-tzu. Tao te ching. I. Title.
BL1900.L35K39 1998
299' .51482—dc21   98-18498
                                                           CIP

Distributed by

USA   Southeast Asia   Japan
Charles E. Tuttle Co., Inc.   Berkeley Books Pte. Ltd.   Tuttle Shokai Ltd.
RR 1 Box 231-5   5 Little Road #08-01   1-21-13, Seki
North Clarendon, VT   Singapore 536983   Tama-ku, Kawasaki-shi
05759   Tel: (65) 280-3320   Kanagawa-ken 214, Japan
Tel: (802) 773-8930   Fax: (65) 280-6290   Tel: (044) 833-0225
Fax: (802) 773-6993   Fax: (044) 822-0413

First edition
1 3 5 7 9 10 8 6 4 2   00 99 98

Design by Vernon Press, Inc., Boston, Massachusetts
Jacket Design by Jill A. Feron
Printed in the United States of America

Introduction

I HAVE GIVEN A GREAT DEAL OF THOUGHT to my reasons for wanting to do an interpretation of the teachings of Lao Tzu. Through martial arts, karate in particular, I have accomplished much in my life, and following those teachings, I have come to understand why a person, having been created, attains his own sense of being.

As I approach my sixtieth year—having studied these things for well over forty of them—I have gone through life tests that accompany any form of enlightenment. I have decided that I should explain what most people consider the hidden meanings of the *Tao Te Ching* to the world, though I, myself, no longer see any hidden meanings. Based on my experiences in life, both good and bad, and my understanding of the *Tao*, it is my joy to pass along what I have learned.

There are countless versions of the *Tao*. This one is written because the truth should be explained without the kinds of intellectual pronouncements that so often accompany this type of work. It is simply a book of poetry and passion. It is a part of my life and it extends from my art, through my art, as my art, and in my art by virtue of what I refer to as the "Spirit of the Thing Itself."

In these pages, my voice is the same as that heard in my training hall and at my seminars. Through these writings I exemplify the passion I hold for these truths. Should I ever falter in my own beliefs, it is because I have not thoroughly understood what I am trying to know. Therefore, you will see no weakness in my tone and you will see no rigidity.

Historically, Lao Tzu lived around 600 B.C. More than likely he is a figment of the minds of sages who did not want to be relegated to positions of wisdom or of being considered mystics. The majority of opinions concerning the man himself are surrounded by myth, but the work, *Tao Te Ching*, has lasted through the ages. It is said by many scholars that Lao Tzu is more than one person and that the *Tao* is a compilation of wisdom that came into being over a great period of time. The words *lao tzu* can be translated literally to mean "old man" or "old philosopher."

Lao Tzu's work consists of eighty-one brief poems. The number eighty-one has no special meaning as far as I can determine. The poems have been translated and reinterpreted over and over again. The poems in this volume are original with only a word or two, now and then, based on other poems that have come before. Each person defines the Tao according to his own understanding. As long as sincerity is the keynote, each one is valid. Some are better than others and, of course, some are not so good. That you come to this particular volume is based on a higher intelligence of the universal consciousness that is the Tao. It should not be questioned.

Over the years many great sages have added their comments to the original work and so mine now join the rest.

It is unnecessary to delve into the actual history of the *Tao Te Ching*. That would only detract from the intent of my interpretation. I give you an understanding of what it is from my point of view. The *Tao* becomes specific to the life of each man and woman when it is followed. In my estimation, everyone is a warrior on one level or another.

Yin and yang, which play a significant part in ancient Chinese philosophy, came into existence somewhere around the third century B.C. They are the opposite of each other and suggest that the middle line, which comes with understanding, is the one to follow if one is to attain perfection in life. However, what is positive to one person is negative to someone else. Knowing this also suggests that there is no such thing as attaining perfection because all is already perfect. It is possible to approximate the ideal of perfection, but the actuality of its realization is beyond human comprehension.

The idea of Taoism is to release your own self from selfishness. The absolute perfect state of enlightenment, which can only be attained through selfishness, is in seeking the self-evident union with the all-masterful God of the universe by letting "things" flow through their own nature. The doctrine is actually quite simple to understand. The only challenge is that you have to divorce yourself from thinking in terms of personal profit—and not only in terms of money. Regardless of your position on earth, abnegation of desire is virtually impossible to attain.

The Tao enables those with a true desire to approximate the universal ideal. By constant repetition of the truths in one's mind, heart, and soul, the ideal can be attained though I have yet to meet someone who has succeeded in attaining it.

Tao is the Way of the universe—the whole universe, every flower and stone. However, it goes much deeper than that. The Way as an explainable thing cannot be the Way at all. The thing that is named is not the thing itself but only the words we use to identify it. The virtue of the Tao means a way to go and to act. There is a great misunderstanding concerning the nature of virtue. It is not to be confused with the Tao itself. It is a notion arising from the intellect that proceeds to bring us to the next higher level of understanding from that previously understood. It is not meant as a direction in a traveling sense but rather as an approach/nonapproach to a higher truth based on our own morality. Understanding comes through language, which is not to be construed as the use of words. It is intuitive language, which though it does not use words, is clearly understood by those wishing to do so. This is based on personal choice and is not confusing when thoughtfully considered.

If a question presents itself as you read, ask yourself that question over and over again. Each time you ask it of yourself expect the answer to be revealed to you through understanding your being-ness. Do not confuse this with knowing God. God is unnameable, at this point in your consciousness, and therefore cannot be known.

The work is straightforward and encompasses every aspect of living, in this world or any other—martial, religious, secular notwithstanding; other planes notwithstanding. It relates to the earthly physical, and the conscious mental as much as it concerns the spiritual. Each of the three is dependent on the others in the human finite condition.

I firmly believe in greater knowledge than I myself can ever come to understand in my finite condition. This greater knowledge, the Spirit of the Thing Itself, is not meant to be a mystical term, but rather it is used to put myself and my reader into a proper frame of reference in relation to the universe.

All interpretations and divulging of profound truths are my own. Any errors I make in my judgment exact their own price in living my life, so there are no excuses. There are no practice sessions. Nor are there time or space limitations. The Tao is an explanation of life, nothing more, nothing less.

I make no distinction in my mind between the sexes. It should be noted that, if one gender is more prevalent than another in the text, it is strictly based on consistency and accepted writing style. Quite frankly, if I were to go into combat with a select battalion, I would prefer it to be composed of women. Why? Though women as well as men can easily take life (perhaps with more ease in certain circumstances), women also nurture it with more understanding and compassion. War would more than likely come to cease sooner.

It is purported that Confucius said, "When the heart and the spirit are weak, man will turn to the higher places and ask for redemption. My prayers have been in place since time immemorial. If they have not, then there is no way to understand the intention of the Universe."

I agree with this Confucian precept. Perhaps my desire to do this work is based on the perceptions of my own ego. Perhaps it isn't. I am wise enough to know that I can pretend to know why I have been chosen by the Spirit of the Thing Itself to be a teacher. I do so because I know I am guided by Heaven.

Stephen F. Kaufman
New York, 1998

1

The true way is unknown and so is the untrue way

There are no names to understand it

Creation does not care that it is the source of creation

It emanates as some "thing"

And is not without nourishment

Mysteries are revealed

Become Its way

Attain Its perfection

Do not use words to describe its no-thing-ness

The three are the same but distinct

One is the Body

One is the Heart

One is the Mind

To understand it as one is the most you can do

It is the path to higher and lesser knowledge

Man cannot know that which is unknowable. At best he can only suggest Its meaning according to his own personal needs. There are no titles he can give to even his own ideas of what this profound truth is except words that still cannot explain Its essence. It cannot be known through an address and cannot be known through no-address. It does not need man's recognition. It forever sustains Itself. The source of creation is not concerned that It is the source of creation. If It were concerned with Itself, It would interfere with Itself. If It interfered with Itself, It would be impure and therefore would never be perfect. This perfect source of perfect creation must come from a perfect source of perfect creation—from the infinite to the finite—back and forth into the no-thing-ness of the conscious universe, Itself.

When we get out of our own way and permit infinite wisdom to express itself through us, it is because we have decided to permit the Spirit of the Thing Itself to dominate us for its own good and our perfection. This is done through acceptance of It. The only way we can understand what is happening to us is by inventing words to describe ourselves to ourselves. Then, we may continue to interact with others until we pass through yin and yang, cease being what we thought we were, and simply become ourselves. Otherwise we must become hermits and not have intercourse with anyone. Otherwise we will be considered mad and have to leave our places.

When we understand that our perfection is based on our own words and finally forgo a description, we can fully express the Spirit of the Thing Itself. We will have stopped using words that limit us or It. To do this, learn words that teach you to overcome desire. This is the ultimate desire.

It is required that a man come to understand the foolishness of "doing" things. Only then can he accurately and with grace "do" things—which is exactly the same matter. Seek never to strike another by completely knowing a strike. Permit your body and mind to extend into the Spirit of the Thing Itself. Take joy in your action without concern for perfection. *That* is perfect.

2

If there is one thing then there is another

If there is good then there is evil

If there is grief then there is joy

If something is beautiful then something is ugly

Neither is more important than the other

Neither exists without the other

All come from the same source

Perceive the words men use

They ignore the source and try to name the Nameless

Perfection simply exists and needs no words

It does not know It is good or evil

It does not care if It is high or low

It is not affected by the words men use to limit themselves

 Nothing is better than anything else except in the mind of man. If you decide that something is good, it is because you have already decided that something else is bad. When you make the conscious choice that all is good you will disavow any negativity and will not experience bad. This is not a simplistic attitude. It is based on infinite intelligence. Why would you want to experience anything bad? Deny it and it will cease to exist in your experience. It must be fully negated.

In the infinite harmony of the universe, man is not intelligent enough to determine relationships leading toward perfection. Your perceptions will never be in accord with the perceptions of others and attempting to make them so will weaken the harmony between you and the work you are trying to do. You should work to understand fully that which you are doing. If in time you find that you are not being granted a personal deliverance through your practice, perhaps what you are doing is not correct for you.

It is the same with learning a new technique without understanding those you are already familiar with. If you think something is better because of its appearance, you are mistaken about the intent of the original technique. It is foolish to try to understand that which is beyond comprehension. It is wise to seek higher understanding by allowing the Spirit of the Thing Itself to take you into Its heart because of your devotion to It.

Work for the sake of accomplishing the task at hand and understanding, in the beginning, the work is more important than the worker. When you finish your task, look at what you have achieved. If you have worked with your heart, you will be pleased with the results. These results should make you want to achieve even more in your next endeavor. The results are the true rewards of a man's labors. It is foolish to try to determine what you think your efforts are worth. This will make you unhappy and will cause you to think incorrectly about the work you are doing. You will begin to overlook essentials and become unhappy. Your profit will gain you nothing.

Perfection knows what It seeks in Itself. It derives energy and spirit as the source of all things. Because It is not concerned with the definitions that man applies to things, It can flow smoothly without disruption or discord. By a simple acceptance of your own perfection, enjoy it as already existing.

3

If a man is not rewarded for his excellence

He will not seek perfection in his work

If things of great luxury are not flaunted

Thieves and murderers will cease to be

A wise man does not boast of his fortune

In front of people less self-blessed

People being content

Will produce more for their masters

Keeping them ignorant they do not know what to strive for

Maintain your vision while doing your work

Keep dominion over your desires

And attain perfection

If you strive to do perfect work and you embody your-self in that work, your efforts will be rewarded. If you do not, you will eventually cease working for the benefits to be derived. Continue to work toward the goal of your own perfection and you are on your way to enlightenment.

You are on your way toward enlightenment. But you will never attain it. Why? Because you are finite in form and therefore cannot comprehend the infinite. That is why there is no such thing as perfect technique. A great deal of luck is based on the amount of practice that has gone into the accomplishment of the endeavor. It is therefore unwise to brag about your accomplishments. In reality they are not yours. Others, seeing your good fortune, will try to relieve you of it and you will have to protect yourself rather than move forward in your work. Don't compete; seek to create with the help of Heaven.

When you attempt to define Heaven, your finite thinking will interfere. The Spirit of the Thing Itself is thereby restricted by your arrogance. It will be unable to produce what it knows is best for you. Attempting to stop impressing your attitude on others is also detrimental to your progress. It is best to stop thinking about what you are doing entirely and simply do it. This does not mean to become unconscious and lackadaisical toward your work. After you see what the results of your efforts are, you can decide to change the direction of the work you are doing to attain the results you desire.

Stop thinking! You are not qualified to do so on the level of the infinite and will only cause yourself grief. Considering the value of another in relation to you leads to envy and jealousy as well because your ego will interfere. Self-aggrandizement is not self-knowing and ego trips will restrict you even further, causing additional confusion and frustration. And so the cycle continues.

4

There is nothing to consider

All things are as one

It does not matter what you think you should do

All things are already done

All things come from one place

Without a parent it exists

Without a child it is all

It is not hungry and wants for nothing

It does not care if you are and do

No difficulty can remain in existence

No problem exists so none need be resolved

It is empty and yet filled

It is never filled and it is never empty

If anything is anything, everything is everything

How can no-thing be described

By not describing it

Think of it and it becomes that

All things are already done and nothing needs to be desired. Yet we continue to seek things we desire, believing they are lacking in our lives. This reasoning is something that we put into our own heads. Things we force ourselves to attain can never be correct because the will needs constantly to be guarded against weakness. Forcing ourselves to attain things can never be correct regardless of appearance. People intuitively know this. Why not know instead that you have everything you want and enjoy the appearance of these things in your life by your acceptance of them as your reality? If you do that, you will be letting go of your own self-imposed thoughts and you will think you are not in control.

What you do not understand is that other people have the same problems as you do. Men seek to attain the goods of others and become devious in their thinking. As a result they also bring unhappiness into their lives, including the attendant frustrations. What a foolish way to live. Be happy with your lot in life. Only then can you build on what you have in order to attain what you desire. If you think you are unable to accomplish a certain deed, you must simply restructure your thoughts about it. Once that is done you can expect a perfect result based on your new thinking. It is the same with being fierce in combat. It is the same with observing an exquisite sunset. It is the same when remembering your last tender kiss.

5

The world appears to be unkind

Filled with generals and others who would

Usurp each and all

Empty promises fill the void

The earth is as a shallow grave

Straw dogs seek recompense

It does not mean they will receive it

Wise men are best unlistened to

Their hearts seem filled with ingratitude

Discussions of right and wrong are neverending

They fill the heavens with meaningless clutter

Each man seeking his own never finds it in another

As all things fill the void with no-thing

It is best to listen to your own heart

Without offering blame

Understand your truth

Never expect others to give you the right to their own hearts regardless of their good intentions—or their apparent weakness. No one is immune to the soul-rending cries of confusion. Each man reaches for Heaven in his own way. When Heaven is asked in the right manner, it gushes forth with all the joy you can accept. When things seem to be at their worst, you should understand that you have to change your approach to the meaning of your own life. Never find faults in others, especially when you are unable to see your own.

If your teacher tells you to do something, listen until you understand. If your teacher does not satisfy your soul then you should seek another, unless you feel you are capable of teaching yourself. At the point where you seek your own counsel, be sure to know your own truth. If you seek justice without a guide, you must not be confused by Divine Right Action.

While Heaven is completely at your disposal, it insists that you be its own but it does not care. When you are in agreement with Heaven, all things are revealed. No longer will you have to consider the opinions of others. Anything of value has no value unless you use it for its purpose by letting it be.

6

The more you take the more It has to give

Never decreasing what the Mother of heaven allots

Approach the gateway

You are more distant

Try not to understand Her secrets

Use Her with the joy She expects

Divine Breath can never be known

A mother's pleasure is her own

The Infinite contains all. The more you take from It the more It has to give. It is foolish to try to use up the resources of the universe. They are neverending and although you approach with good intentions you will still be farthest away. Man can never understand the machinations of the universe and must always consider newer truths to be learned. Like a mother, it will give nourishment to all who desire sustenance; it will give it gladly, as that is the nature of a mother.

When you try to take your abilities to the ultimate level of accomplishment, you will find that you have really learned little about the possibilities provided. This is because you think you have attained the level of Its most givingness. If you try to get all there is to get you will find that there is always more to strive for. In time you will stop enjoying the fruits of your labors and become blinded to the pleasures of life. Always know when you have enough, though you will never know when you have as much as another. It is not true that the man with the most possessions wins. The winner is the man with all the possessions. When do you know if you have enough? Your heart will tell you.

Divine Breath pervades the allness of everything. Man is limited by his finiteness and can never comprehend eternity. The nature of Heaven though, cannot resist giving of Itself to know more of Itself through you. Heaven must be acknowledged and then approached with sincerity. You can never expect results if you think in terms of false pride, arrogance, or conceit. Rid yourself of these restrictions with a sincere desire to do so.

7

Death does not exist and only reveals nextness

Wisdom does not permit the end of itself

A man can only learn to move forward in any direction

Not being concerned with what went before

He should not care for the rewards of the day

Seeking only that which can enhance his own reality

He does not consider the rewards of his work

By not considering the results of his work

They are perfect and cannot be made better

When you strive to develop an aspect of yourself to the ultimate degree, you are still limited by your perception of what that level of beingness actually can be. It is not possible to understand the workings of the universe because the universe has its own idea about its own being. It does not concern itself with its own being. If it did, it would not be unending. In order to attain the highest level of all consciousness, a man must be concerned only with doing the best that can be done, limited only by his mind and the acceptance of a higher truth of himself. This is called "death of the past."

Nextness is what happens after a man leaves his body, or that which was behind him, not caring to carry it along to his next destination on earth or anywhere else. When nextness is reached, allness is released according to the conventions a man uses in his own thinking through personal contemplation of the Spirit of the Thing Itself. All is accomplished because the Spirit of the Thing Itself is expressed to the level of the man's ability to understand and accept its profound gifts. These gifts are made manifest in the world as a result of a man's work and his desire to attain perfection. If a man is enlightened, he will see these things as something beyond what he could ever imagine.

This must not be confused with objects of physical possession that can be touched and held. These are only things that, in time, will cease to be in the form they now possess. Imperfection exists only because man cannot identify the Spirit of the Thing Itself as the means of Heaven's and man's natural existence. Heaven and man must coincide with each other. They must be the same.

8

Water will seek its own level
It is the nature of water to do so
Unrestricted by the opinions of rocks in the stream
It goes where it will and is patient to do so

Man must ascend to his own level of accomplishment
This is the truth of accomplishment as perceived by man
If his desire denies his reception
He must rethink his dream
If he insists that Heaven unfold for him
It may or may not according to his belief

No blame can be placed
Some are masters and others are masters

If a man excels at his craft and still does not attain perfection, it is because he has not accepted the perfection of the Spirit of the Thing Itself. You are truly capable of understanding the universe and all of its possibilities from your finite perspective. When a man seeks to do the very best he can conceive of doing, there is no reason for him to find fault with the work he is doing and certainly not with the work anyone else is doing. Perfection has nothing to do with speed and nothing to do with strength. If he is still unable to attain it by continued concentration on the goal, perhaps the goal is not clearly defined in his heart.

Just because a man desires to accomplish something, it does not mean that he will. His purpose may not be correct under Heaven. The universe, being entirely impersonal, has no reason not to grant a man his wishes exactly according to his desire. Understanding this leads to sublime peace. It also enables a man to accomplish more than he could ever imagine.

The Way to understand all is simply to develop the desire to understand more. By right of consciousness, accept all there is to receive from the boundless supply of the universe. The only means by which the universe can ever know itself is by man's desire to have more of the Spirit of the Thing Itself open and reveal more on a personal basis. To think any other way is completely erroneous. The more of himself a man accepts as a direct extension of Heaven, the more Heaven can admit to being.

All men are masters of their own reality. No one is more in tune with Heaven than anyone else. People need only believe they are extensions of universal intelligence and they become that much more than they acknowledge of themselves. Man is his own master. Circumstance does not withhold anything truly desired.

9

Though you have and hold you still do not possess

To maintain control you must let things go

If your house is filled with treasures

Your sleep is always uneasy

You do not know when strangers will approach

Take all you can and fill your coffers with gold

Throwing it back to the crowd be sure to increase your lot

When you have attained fortune and fame

Retire from the world

Enjoy your new ease and grace

This is the way of the wise

It does not make sense to continue hoarding after you have enough. People will see you as rapacious and will attempt to relieve you of the burden of your wealth. In the arena of competition, the same applies to one who would suggest to others that he is the master of reality. If you win a prize, you must first continue your devotion to the source that provided it to you. More ease and grace will appear in your life and you will continue in the path of understanding. Not to do so indicates a lack of your responsibility to the Spirit of the Thing Itself. When you lose your connection to the universe, you will see that the Spirit of the Thing Itself has lost its connection to you.

To avoid the embarrassment of false pride, arrogance, and conceit, focus on releasing your need to prove yourself to anyone or anything. Devotion to the Spirit of the Thing Itself will increase Its desire to reveal more of Itself to you. How simple it is to live in the embrace of Heaven while treading your daily path. When you accomplish much you should understand that it is time for you to go to the mountain and express your life with pleasure and ease and never in the face of the enemy—who may not even know he is your enemy until he becomes aware of your possessions. Never permit anyone to know your level of knowing. They will blame you for their failure.

10

Is the mystic virtue necessary to be known

Can you find yourself as the taker and the giver

Without thought of reward

Be the woman and the man

You will love and govern without consideration

Feed your children

Do not tell them it is your food

Live in the world and not be of it

Care for but do not possess

Lead without leading

Benevolence without indication

Leads to the gates of Heaven

What must a man do to be in control of his own destiny and at the same time be in the hearts of his people without their knowing that he is there? When distinction is made between acts and duties, the need for personal reward arises. Devotion to reward will always interfere with the result of your labors. Is it important to be praised by others when they see your skills? Or is it better to be praised by Heaven for your devotion to it? Do not be coerced by the thoughts of others into thinking that the work you do is yours without cause. When you are devoted to Heaven you are protected as the messenger of its own purpose. In such a way can you be delivered from heartbreak.

It is essential that you depend on nothing but the higher self, which is truly your lover. It is the female and male without distinction. To truly understand taking, you must be of a giving nature. To give with sincerity is the essence of true takingness. Giving yourself to your work you will take into your heart the mystery of its own substance. If there is not gladness of heart in a man's giving and taking there can never be harmony and balance. All will always be lost. The gates of Heaven are only the gates of Heaven. What you find upon entering is more than you ever could conceive of. This is the Way of life—that you always acknowledge the source of your being. In this way the Spirit of the Thing Itself will never forsake you.

11

The wheel is useless without the space between the spokes

The walls of the house contain the useful space

Clay pots do not contain water in their structure

Only in the space between

It is not the hand that caresses

It is the space that feeling embraces

It is the sound of the flute and not the flute itself

No matter how strong the edifice you build, no matter how powerful you make your body and your mind, no matter how well you craft your work, its form is only valued for the amount of no-thing-ness that remains between the obvious parts. The ideas to craft the project come from the unseen and they are only understood when the seen is observed as surrounding and being surrounded by no-thing. This is God, the Void, and this is what must be understood by a man before he can be consider himself wise. The wise man understands that his own mind is based on no-thing-ness revealing itself to him personally and directly. It still does not show its face.

Even that which is poorly crafted is built according to the desires of the man making it. Perfection is based on devotion and nothing else. Devotion to the final result comes from man's ardent desire. Even when a man does not accept the beneficence of Heaven he is still under the direct control of his thoughts. Thoughts are the emanations and province of Heaven. Before starting out on a project, the thoughts exist that permit the product to be built. It cannot be otherwise. The reality of the unseen permits man to have the thought and, even if a man suggests that he is his own creator, he must still acknowledge his own being. It is Heaven that has always existed and always will—never having begun and never having ended.

12

Senses deaden the spirit

Sounds of pleasure are discordant

The soundless sound and the colorless color

Reveal the truth of what they are

The goods men derive from their conquests drive them

Mad for more they are slowed down

Never attaining the reality of their quest

Wise men select that which is correct

Not permitting mind to interfere

 Sensual enjoyment of goods is a passing thing and must not be relied upon for eternal gratification. Eventually your senses will need more for satisfaction. When thoughts about instant gratification arise, things lose their essence. The wise man understands this and comes to see that the only thing that does indeed matter is the scent of the rose and the beauty that its form provides. This is a personal consideration at best. Understanding the structure of the rose perhaps enables a man to see into its nature and he can therefore refine his own perceptions to evoke more expression from the flower itself. Without knowing that the Spirit of the Thing Itself is responsible for his thoughts, a man will create monsters that do nothing to enhance the joy of his world.

If your technique is such that you can be the ultimate in performance according to other men, do not permit yourself to think you have attained the ultimate goal of your actions. This will cause your growth to stop. You will become boring—first to yourself and then to others. You then will try to be what others think you should be, which will further deny what you can truly express yourself as. At the same time, do not become presumptuous and think you are the only thing on the earth or that you are God. Even though you are, you must first come to understand that everyone else is that also.

For this reason, a man must learn to control his thoughts. If he does not, all of his past thinking will reflect in the new expression of his desires with all the perfection of imperfection. Mind can only work though a man's mind based on what it knows about the desires expected of it. Consider the development of the soul as a direct extension of the Spirit of the Thing Itself, which will permit the manifestation of more freedom of choice. It will provide you with new ideas that can only enhance your experience while you are in finite form.

Always praise Heaven. By your devotion to it you will find more than you ever could have imagined demonstrating as utter perfection. This is the Way of Heaven.

13

Only he should rule

Who understands all people are the same

Only he should rule

Who loves all men as himself

Only he should rule

Who understands the unity of separateness

Bestowed with pride he falls from Heaven's grace

From disgrace he arises owning nothing but himself

Owning nothing he gives with an open heart

To be in favor and to be in disgrace are the same

To fall from favor and be lifted from disgrace are the same

A man who sees the difference sees the same thing

He who does not see the same thing is confused by both

Wishing to be availed of only favor

Expecting the bounty of the Universe

To not show him special favor

His special favor is himself

The egotism involved with ascent through arrogance, conceit, and false pride is such that guard must be taken against its expression. The more you practice to become a perfect example of all, the easier is acceptance of the Divine Beauty of all life. When loss of position comes, it is difficult for the man who thinks his rank was granted by himself to reassert his position in the world. Seeing rank as an extension of his own mind, he understands that there is never anything to lose because there was never anything to be gained. He is at peace with himself and walks in harmony with every man. He uses the value of his rank to become even more valuable to the Spirit of the Thing Itself.

The wise man gives with an open heart knowing that all is granted from Heaven as a special gift that he desires to experience. Should he lose his composure about such things he will quickly fall into the depths of terror, brought about by his own thinking, that he is all that matters. Lifting himself from this morass of negativity, he sees the specialness of nothing except himself and he is able to guide himself and to guard his domain without effort.

Being a man of wisdom, he sees being special as holding nothing of merit and does not become vulnerable. He understands that he can be trusted. Even though his rank and authority are treated as extensions of his own soul, he can walk in peace knowing that the hideous weight of responsibility is governed only by Heaven, and that his acknowledgment of it is what protects the realm of his mind. His burden to himself vanishes and he lives in joy.

14

It is elusive—It cannot be touched

It is audible—yet cannot be heard

It is exquisite—yet It cannot be sensed

It is form before being formless

It is reality before being thought

It does not shine when It rises

It does not subside when It rests

Being without any causation It simply is

And has no idea of Itself

It grows and expands or It does not

When the warrior wields his sword it is not with the intention of demonstrating skill, but with the intention of accomplishing the end as he perceives it. The skill involved is a result of his perception of perfection relative to using the sword itself. Some men call this "the void" and say it is emptiness. Yet it is filled with every thought that ever existed or will exist. Timelessness does not control its being. Spacelessness fills every place. The finite understanding of time and space is a limiting factor and has nothing to do with true growth and life.

When you attempt to describe the void, you fail to understand what it is because what you think it is, it isn't. If we were to know that there is nothing to know and we accepted ourselves as the completeness of the universe, we would be without fear forever. Except in the mind of man, lack and limitation simply do not exist. Nor does definition.

15

The land was filled with wisdom

Men understood the unknown

Powers were not strange and dark and foreboding

Yet to those with them—all light

Never were they understood

Crossing the icy stream with measured steps

Playing flutes while walking through danger

Dignified and with great politeness

Ready for the great unknown

Ecstatic with the joy of being

Never feeling remorse

They ventured forth

Maintaining perfect being

Knowing they were not themselves

In ancient days wise men were never confused as to their proper places. They never rushed about and they never concerned themselves with meaningless profit. They never reveled in another's misfortune. They simply existed and were at one with themselves because there was no need to be anything else. This attitude enabled them to have the wisdom they needed and to be who they were without worrying about being someone else. They never needed renewal in any aspect of their being.

It is the same with a man today: He should not strive to be more than he is and never to be less than he actually is. He should know that all is a result of his thinking. Regardless of where he wants to go, he should never desire to be where another is, but should instead seek those qualities of the divine for himself, accepting them as his own. He should also know the difference between right and wrong as well as the penalties for improper behavior in his society. Changing location, he should seek understanding of his new place. This is called the "harmony of intelligence."

It is wise to acknowledge God as being man and not man being God. Living his life as God, man transcends the need to usurp other men. Not interfering with his divine right, he lives in peace and harmony with all men. Not seeking to rule, he is not ruled. Heaven as ruler and ruled graces his life with happiness.

16

Complete humility
Utter humbleness
Hold steady and be still

The Universe knows
What It wants you to be as It
So you think
You can never understand Its motivations

No thing is total without complement
Do not deceive yourself with false knowing
Accept your fate as the beingness of you yourself
Accept freedom of yourself as total being
Do not confuse the two
They are the same

 All things work together; nothing functions without reference. Your own thoughts have no value if you accept
another's thinking as your own. Being still within permits

a man to express himself fully without having to avoid the limitations imposed by his attempting to think of a higher reality. This is why you should be humble before Heaven. This is why you should express humility beneath the power of Heaven.

It is best to consider the direction in which you think you are going, then release the Spirit of the Thing Itself to express itself. If you seek guidance from Heaven, it will be revealed to you in your thoughts, actions, and deeds. There is no way ever to determine the best manner for something to take place. Only the nameless can be nameless.

When you attempt to control the functions of society and think you are in proper perspective you must be completely detached from it and from the results of it. If you do not, you will interfere with the perfect expression of your own ideal. Learn to trust the unknowable. What you are as being will never cease to be.

Fate and free will are based on knowing your true self. It is not important that you think you are free to choose that which you choose to experience. Neither is it important to think that things happen, because they simply do. You are not God, God is you. Both are the same.

17

The good leader is never seen

The good leader never seeks praise

The good leader is ever sought after

People will do work they are praised for

People will do work they are doing themselves

People will follow the man who does not lead them

The wise man respects all before him

The wise man admires the work of all

The wise man acclaims himself

Knowing it is Heaven's grace

Good teachers reveal what is already known

A leader must know what he desires to accomplish and then delegate that desire to Heaven to be fulfilled. He must remain apart from the people so they cannot come to know him personally. He must understand that the absolute can only accomplish its means through itself. This is very hard for a man to understand and do in the beginning of his studies. But he must strive for it if the project is to be completed in perfection. Then the people can take pride in their work.

The wise teacher does not instruct his students; instead he shows them that they already know what work is to be done. He facilitates their tasks by praising his students for their efforts, so they do their work with glad hearts, not having to impress the master. The teacher does everything that the students are required to do. He may do these things differently and must accept that the students are able to accomplish their own destinies by means of the Spirit of the Thing Itself, without his having to impose his will on them. They become themselves and do not appear to be replicas of the teacher. If the teacher needs to be replicated, the teacher does not know his responsibility to his students. Thus the teacher learns how and what to teach.

18

There was no confusion in life

The Way of righteousness was known

Soon came differences and values

Man lost the Way

Not in harmony with nature

Attitudes were learned to compete with others

Right and wrong began to exist

Nothing was correct

When man first began to consider differences in things, he became opinionated. Then began the great descent. When things were left to their own natures, there was never a problem with getting along. When wisdom and folly were thought about, when love and hate were determined, when intelligence and stupidity were defined, man lost the Way. The only manner in which to regain the state of ultimate bliss is to let the nature of the universe hold sway, by not interfering with the causation of the Spirit of the Thing

Itself. Until that happens, man will be unable to trust his fellows and therefore unable to trust in Heaven's Way.

Conflict exists because a man thinks he is more righteous than another. This leads to ignorance. This leads to war. This leads to pain. This leads to death. This leads to Heaven. This leads to perceived righteousness. This leads back to ignorance. And so the cycle continues.

It is best to ask Heaven for all things knowing that what is desired already exists. His desire will be made whole without needing acceptance from others.

19

Destroy the men of wisdom
Stop teachers in their tracks
Let the people go to their homes
Without the fear of right and wrong

They know what they must do
They do what they know
They want their bellies filled
They want their children covered at night

Banish the profiteers
Abolish the need for judiciality
Then the people will go their Way
Knowing what is correct, what is incorrect

They will not be concerned with the outcome of misdeeds
None will exist

Most people are not interested in the sayings of the supposed great and wise men of ancient times or in the opinions of modern sages. People are interested only in being able to live their lives without difficulty while enjoying the fruits of their labors. That is wisdom enough for any man. When others seek to impose rules and regulations, the free man will, by his very nature, seek to overthrow the authority that he did not desire in the first place. He does this in ways of silence and in ways of noise. Kings would be wise to understand the need to govern from afar, if in fact they have to govern at all. Ignorance is indeed bliss and should never be based on what another decides is yet another's ignorance.

20

Be done with the need to place the fork properly
It is better to enjoy the food and the company

It does not matter that I categorize this
You categorize that
Make no distinction between good and evil
Both will cease to exist

By thinking I am a fool
You will think you are more learned than I
You will refuse me the pleasure of life
You will not permit me to eat
You will not permit me to think
You will not permit me to love

Doing this you destroy yourself
More concerned with controlling me
Than in enjoying your own self

There are more directions than the eight

They reach places you do not know exist

And yet they do

When a man seeks to control others he jeopardizes his own pleasure and joy. He pays for this insolence with grief and anguish and all other things that rob his life of pleasure. Seeking to overcome his pain, he will continue to think that the acquisition of material goods will afford him a better life. He does not realize that those who follow him will be in constant intrigue over who will retain his goods once he dies.

There is never a need to compete. There is only a need to create. Competition is caused by man's inadequacy in using the Spirit of the Thing Itself. Creation continues regardless of what man thinks. That is why the greatest inventions will, in time, cease to exist and machines will be unnecessary. Yet all things will be done.

The nameless is eternal in all directions including the eight you do not know of. These eight directions are non-existent and therefore cannot be identified. Why are they suggested? To give you the truth of never understanding that which cannot be named. It is not difficult to understand this. Just think about the things you do not know.

Machines are merely devices that man invents to make his life more pleasurable. When man comes to understand the truth, he will no longer need false extensions of his spirit, and machines will no longer need to exist. Thought will be all.

When practicing your chosen discipline, never become satisfied with your present understanding of the actions you perform. Practice to become one and the same with what it is you are trying to accomplish. This is the true path to enlightenment. Eventually you will see yourself doing familiar things in a completely new manner. You will be frightened, perhaps, thinking you have lost certain aspects of your own self, but in reality you will be performing in accordance with a higher ideal. This is growth toward Heaven.

21

What need have I to know of the origin of all things

There is no origin of all things except that which I perceive

What need have I of explanations of others

I know the truth of it all is simply the truth of it all

Without definition and without claim

It is elusive because it is without explanation

It changes images according to whim

Or it does not

Without thinking of perfection

I am that

Man lives in the world and is part of it. At the same time, he is not of it. He is the effect of Heaven's causation. Perhaps he is not. When a man seeks to determine his own destiny, he can only describe the universe according to his own personal needs. This is as it should be. When a man accepts the universe on those terms, he ceases needing explanations about anything. If anything is anything, then everything is everything. It is very simple. It is not necessary to seek deliverance when, in truth, deliverance is at hand.

A technique cannot be called one thing and then another. It is simply a technique. When a man releases self-imposed thoughts about it, he will find he is merely the instrument that delivers the technique and not the technique itself. Only then can he determine what the technique actually is. The Spirit of the Thing Itself is all, and as everything reveals itself according to a man's desire. For this reason, a man appears foolish when he considers it necessary to imagine an object in front of him instead of his very own self.

22

He does not compete
Therefore no one competes with him

He yields and therefore does not break
He stands firm in the wind and bends
Accepting no dirt he gives none

He does not display himself
He does not flaunt his riches
No one can take what they do not know he has
And having all that he accepts all the rest

His flame endures with no wick
His flame is from the unknown
The Eternal showers him with grace
Coming to terms and embracing It
The Spirit loves him as he loves himself

There is nothing for which to compete. When men do compete, it is for the express desire of having control over others. To have control, men will do whatever they think is necessary to win. By doing that, they lose the Way. Establishing themselves as controllers, they do not have their own minds. Yet a man may be considered dull witted by other men because he does not seek to control others. It is difficult enough to control your own thoughts, though you presume to be closer to God than I. It is not important to become more of God, nor is it important to be closer to God. It is important to accept more of God.

A man of knowledge does not have to throw his personal self in the faces of others. By keeping his own counsel he maintains his true position under Heaven. By understanding that he is in possession of all he desires, he continuously teaches himself to accept more of the bounty of the universe without fear that others will try to wrest it from him.

When he knows that he can have whatever he wants whenever he wants it, he will appear to be governed by something beyond the understanding of ordinary men. As he comes to understand more of himself in relation to the Eternal Creative Spirit, he will know that more and more grace is being lavished upon him.

Do not confuse universal love of self with an emotional connection to another person. True love is without connection to anything tangible. Knowing my place in the universe, I can only love that which I know as me. When I know who I am, I can truly love myself and will have no problem loving another—living or dead, according to my definition. If you do not love yourself, how can you truly love me? And if you truly love me, you do not have to explain yourself because, as I truly love myself, I am aware of your love through my own.

23

Wind does not blow forever

Rains eventually cease

This is the Way of things

They start

They stop

They never begin

They never end

Whoever would follow the Way of the Tao

Would know they are complete and without doubt

Feeling complete there is no stress or strain

Life goes on and does not complain

If the power of the universe is wrongly used

It will laugh in the user's face

It is wise to honor others

They will therefore honor you

Do not seek it

The truth of nature is that it has its own idea of itself. It does not need permission from man to exist. But it will comply with man's desire. This is so, and a man should always demand more of himself. The more he demands of himself, the more Heaven will reveal and the easier his life will become. If he does not do this, it is because he is not part of what is much more real than his own reality. He is lost and is therefore frightened. Still Heaven gives him what he desires.

When a man follows the Way of the universe without imposing his own misguided will upon it and expresses with true desire that which he truly wants, the universe has no option but to comply with its own nature—that of constant creation. This is hard for men to understand because they are surrounded by what they *think* is correct and not by what they know is correct.

In the same way, if you want others to recognize you for what you truly are, then you must recognize them. Not to recognize another indicates nonacceptance of either yourself or the other. Notice with joy the wonderfulness of others and they will notice the same in you. Do not, however, go out of your way to produce the results you think you deserve. It is better to produce the results you know you deserve by letting them appear in your life as already done.

24

Standing on your toes

You cannot walk aright

You lose balance

Telling others of your adventures

They soon become bored

Bored they breed distrust

Giving them cause to take your goods

Patting your own back

You cannot work with two hands

Your labor is only half

The Spirit of the Thing Itself will not laugh

It knowing you not knowing

The fool you are will be

Blinded by the vision

Standing on your toes may be of value for a small time but eventually you must keep your feet on the ground.

Standing on your toes will permit you to see things farther away than you normally would but in order to attain the reality of those visions you must come back to earth. Better to let the work develop itself, with you as the vehicle for its self-expression. By enjoying the labor of your effort, the work will express itself even more kindly. Admiration by others for the work done is not the pat on the back you are really seeking. When you ascend to that level of self-realization you will become more aware of the weight of responsibility, which will be no burden.

Bragging intimidates people and makes them envy you with the result that they will try to interfere with your projects. They will tell you what you should do to make things better, but this is only according to their perceptions. On the other hand you should not desire to do things that only appear to be of value. This interferes with sensibility.

By not patting yourself on the back you can concentrate even farther ahead to the ultimate reality of your goals. This is called minding your own business. If you surrender yourself to your work, others will have no choice but to know that you know God. Don't let that overwhelm you with false pride. It is a terrible thing to lose the respect of Heaven in all directions including the eight that are unknown.

25

Something was before you were

Formless and complete

Ever more than the void can be

It is all that and nothing more

Not what you perceive It to be

It is the Mother of the world at least

I can not-name It

I can not-see It

I can not-hear It

I can not-feel It

I can not-taste It

It is all that I am

Meaningless words regard It

I understand It completely

It does not wish to be known

The Way is not to be construed as a "thing." That would be naming it and would bring about its decline. To not understand it is to realize that it is beyond comprehension. That is the understanding. In such a manner, know the nameless. The only way to attach to it is through unattachment. The earth and the firmament are the thing itself. You must acknowledge your perfection before your perfection will acknowledge you without insisting on naming the nameless and sensing the senseless.

Practicing with all your heart and soul focused on completion of the goal, you will cause the goal to appear before you and you will know it. It is entirely important to understand technique before you can understand technique. This is not a play on words. It is the truth of understanding yourself as the vehicle for expression of the Spirit of the Thing Itself. This comes with time. How much time? As much as you say. But that does not mean instant demonstration until you understand instant demonstration.

26

The balance of things depends
Upon lightness and weight
The loudest man is silent

Not separated from his goods
He travels the realm
Not permitting his view to block his vision

He rules ten thousand men
Not celebrating but praising
Or considered lightminded
The people will seek another master

It is not good to remain attached to goods of any kind. This includes remaining attached to another person to whom love may appear to be the claiming virtue. Likewise, a man should not tell others of his love or his lover. It will cause jealousy among those less fortunate. A man in control of his destiny will understand the difference between partaking in the frivolity of the people and enjoying the fruits of his labors.

He keeps close watch on his destination and does not permit appearances to alter his direction. Enjoying the pleasures of the people, he praises them and encourages them to accomplish more with the same ease as he, but he does not become one of them or associate in the houses of those not in his court.

In this way he is able to move in the direction of Heaven's desire and will not become lost due to foolish behavior. The strength of the king must be understood to include all those he governs as well. The people must know and believe that his word is sacred. His word must be fulfilled without hesitation or deviation. If the people fail to show him respect, he is wise to seek counsel with Heaven in order to regain his position, meting out punishment where and when it is required. If he continues in the way of frivolity and madness, the people will come to despise him.

It is foolish to express your skills to impress the crowd. Contests between men are just contests between men. They accomplish nothing. They will cause you to lose the true value of your work by only considering the entertainment of other men.

27

The mightiest warrior leaves no trace of destruction

The swiftest runner leaves no trace of footsteps

The grandest poet wastes no words

Nothing to do with good or evil

A perfect star is impossible to touch

Do not think virtue is only good

So-called bad is also perfection

Wise men will know that unwise men are not always fools

A fool knows that a wise man can be beneficial to him

Except in thought, there can be no such thing as the absolute on the finite plane. It is wise to rid yourself of the relative when discussing the infinite. When true perfection is attained there is no difference. What would be the value of knowing the difference if one does not exist?

It is the same with men when they try to determine the difference between the yin and the yang, good or bad, right or wrong. Knowing that both are connected by reality, a man of thought and wisdom will know as well that there is no need for either. There is no such thing as yin and yang. This is not to suggest that yin and yang do not exist.

Many so-called evil men have done wondrous things for the people. As the reverse is true, the good that men presume to do can visit everyone with great turmoil. Go about your business and if you prefer to be a warrior, be a warrior, but know what a warrior is. The ultimate aim of the warrior is to live in peace and not to practice his art. This is called enlightenment.

28

As you are masculine so are you feminine

Filled with joy you must know emptiness and despair

To be one thing you must know the opposite

Then you can perceive the value of choice

Preferring light know the darkness

Thinking through life understand the value of death

If there is one there is another

They are both the same

When you see a man's glory

Know that he has also had shame

Immune to either or

To be one thing know the other

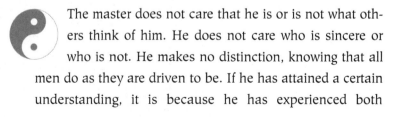 The master does not care that he is or is not what others think of him. He does not care who is sincere or who is not. He makes no distinction, knowing that all men do as they are driven to be. If he has attained a certain understanding, it is because he has experienced both

aspects of reality. It is not possible to understand one aspect of the universe without having experienced the other. It is the way of nature to be known to its children. When you have experienced both, you may make the conscious choice of living one way or another. Not before.

The sword is not the man. The man is not the sword. They both exist to be the thing itself. Whatever that thing is, that you decide it to be. Having never known defeat you can never know victory—and then only to the extent you have known it. Make no distinction between victory and defeat and in this way always be unbeatable. In life you will always see things as they appear until you know what they are. You may at times be envious. This is natural until you come to understand that each man is his own savior.

29

Thinking you can take the world

Shaping it to your own desire

You are mistaken

It will not last

The earth is its own thing and will serve its own nature

If you try to change it

It will laugh in your face

If you try to spoil it

Time will transcend your being

Not to mention Heaven Itself

Which will not even laugh or know that you tried

Things move forward things move back

It is the Nature of Things

Not of Heaven

Not knowing time space or motion

Never will the sane man

Expect the world to do his bidding

Expect Heaven to part on his behalf

Work in harmony with all being-ness

And reap the rewards thereby

Regardless of the power and strength of anyone who has gone before, the changes they wrought have not remained intact through the ages because changes are measured in time. Man can foul his place and throw his debris into the sky but it will not remain. Change necessitates invention and invention is required for change. That is why the body changes and shifts with age. What was strength becomes power to the wise. What was speed must become quickness, also to the wise. Better to know this when you are a youth expecting pleasure to come with ease and grace.

Heaven knows what It must do for Its own enjoyment. Perhaps indulging a man now and then and perhaps not, It does what It wants done and although offering suggestions to all people, still It directs Its ownness.

We are Heaven's pawns regardless of our self-esteem and only reap the joy we can accept. Heaven does not know good or evil. It only knows perfection.

30

The wise counselor advises the ruler

Against the use of arms

Men cost more than the weapons they choose

Governed through fear the land turns to chaos

The people will despise the king

The wise general knows when to march and when to halt

Knowing when to rest his troops

When to force them onward

He understands their value

When they must be fed

When they must be entertained

When they must be rewarded

When they must be punished

A wise man attaining that which he sought for

Does not make more of victory than it is worth

The accomplishment of a goal

Is the accomplishment of the goal

To force it to produce more than it should invites disaster

If you would command troops, you must know their value and use them properly. You must know when to advance your men and when to restrain them. If you delegate the realm to another, that person will see its growth or demise according to his desire rather than the needs of the people. This will cause you to lose control as well as the throne. Once your goal is attained, you should proceed further along your path of desire and not force temporary conditions to subject themselves to what you think because of your ego.

Thinking erroneously causes teachers to lose students. It makes rulers lose their domains. Forgetting the nature of the goal, they forget that their students and subjects were the vehicle for attainment of the goal. When the teacher has done his work, he must release the child to be the man.

Wisdom comes with age and experience—not before. A person should have a desire for great knowledge when still a youth. Attaining it and then, understanding it, he will accomplish many great things further on in life. Sometimes he is wrong and must be able to make his changes in stride. There is nothing incorrect in making change for the ideal of the goal, but never for the value sought from personal gain.

31

Understand the folly of war

Understand the value of life

Attaining success also attains grief

In times of strife wise men too will turn to evil

They protect their world without regard to cost

'Til turning back to the Way they seek redemption

Wise men also enter into conflict at various times. It must be understood that they, too, are human. If they are truly wise they will quickly know that they will have to return to the Way in time. Such a deviation wastes time and interferes with the evolution of the Divine Ideal since it has been thwarted in Its expression by ignorance and self-proclaimed evil. But, at times, even this is necessary to grow. Why change at all? It is simpler to think in terms of universal harmony at all times and never to have to resort to other means that certainly are not in line with Heaven. If a man delights in harming another, how can he think he is virtuous? True virtue cannot be explained by personal value. It must be understood in relation to the rest of the universe of which man is part. If a man is not part of the universe, then he simply does not exist.

What a malady: The intention of Heaven is unknowable. Perhaps chaos rules in the infinite, perhaps it does not. There is no way to know Heaven's Way, even when we see those things that would suggest we do. Conflict and war only bring heartbreak and destruction, which are never excuses for growth. If something is renewed, it is thought to have been alterable. To reason this intuitively is not the same as understanding growth through change. If you seek to improve your lot in life through combative methods, you do not correctly perceive the value of understanding life. Your lot grows naturally when you accept it is a natural extension of your perceptions. If you do not accept the reality of Heaven, it is better to play solitaire and consider the events in your life based on a turning of the cards.

32

The Universe is Unnameable

It will never be understood

If It were then It would not be unfathomable

Man would know Its name and It would not need to exist

Adhering to the Way

All is given with Eternal gladness

Without desire It knows not lack loss or limitation

Kings control the matters at hand

Bringing rules

Unhappiness and grief result

Conflict does not confuse Heaven

It does not know right or wrong

Good and evil come to exist

People go hungry and children cry in the night and day

Men fear the unknown. They fear it because they cannot understand what it portends and so think it is death. They differentiate between living and dying, and not wanting to realize that both are components of life itself, they quell their fears by seeking control over others who are generally uncontrollable.

How foolish for a man to think he can devise rules for the world to follow so that he himself can gain enlightenment. This is impossible. There are as many ideas about perfection as there are people. When you force people to change their customs because you think you are better than they, you will cause them to turn against you and devise your demise, even if they first appear to be following you. Because you have attempted to take away their spirit, they will revolt with fierce determination and will injure themselves because of you. A man who desires this is not wise.

Heaven is not concerned with what a man considers right or wrong. Heaven creates according to the desire of everyone—individually and collectively. When foolishness prevails, all the people suffer, including the king. The breakdown in order will bring with it a lack and limitation that goes against the natural harmony of abundance.

33

To know the Ways of others is knowledge
To know one's Self is wisdom

Conquering himself he is powerful
Conquering others he is only strong

Long life lasts forever based on one's deeds
To perish means you have thought only of yourself

There is a profound difference between power and strength, though most people confuse the two. Power is a gift from the Eternal based on devotion to the Spirit of the Thing Itself. Strength, too, is wrought by Heaven, but it does not last because a man will never be able to maintain his strength in old age. Power will always exist because it is the nature of the universe.

When a man has conquered himself, he now has the ability to direct Heaven according to his true desire. This is a good thing. Man is able to select the experience he will have on earth. This is the gift of Heaven.

If you spend all your time conquering others, what will you attain except for vainglorious empathy from the people? What will you conquer for yourself? You will cease to exist anyway and your memory will not give your descendants rest. Better to have lived and passed in peace than to live in infamy and have your children rue the day of your birth.

34

Greatness spreads Its wealth without restriction

Always more to be had there is never lack of supply

There is never a need to want

The Spirit of the Thing Itself is not concerned

With what it has or does not have

Including that which does not exist

Attempt to understand that which is ununderstandable

Man can not accept Universal Love

And not bow down

In humility before It

Praising It ever higher and higher

How is it possible even to attempt to conceive of understanding the unknowable? To do so would mean that total wisdom expressed itself in you and it would be unnecessary to live a life on earth. You would be the Infinite—which of course, you are. You just have not accepted the fact that you are. There is unlimited abundance of all, everywhere, known and unknown.

This may be what happens in the state of what man calls "death." That state is not understandable either from an earthly point of view. Do not believe the magicians. It is important to understand that wisdom will reveal only that which needs to be revealed at the time of genuine change in consciousness of man as desired by a man. Ask for it and you may be fortunate or unfortunate to receive it. It would be best to not consider it at all.

When you are in deep contemplation of ascending to your heart's ultimate desire, keep your mind focused on the Divine Ideal. You are then in complete humility, and Heaven must respond because that is Its nature. It is a giving nature and because it is giving, you must feed it with love and devotion to yourself, which it acknowledges as itself, thereby releasing all of its abundance into your life as you define it—your life.

Praise It. Praise It. Praise It. Unceasingly.

35

Life shines in your face

Know you are blessed

Know you are blessed

Life shines in your face

Seek music not only from instruments

Nor pictures from an artist's canvas alone

To do so restricts the beauty of the universe

Expressing itself through all

Spirit extends through you

Use it and appreciate its use

More is revealed to you personally

It is never anything to see or feel

Or taste or sense or hear

And can only be known by knowing it

 Every time you try to define something, a need to further identify that which you are trying to define will
always arise: You are afraid of losing that which you

only think you know. In this manner the goal is never attained. Because spirit cannot be known, it is all things. You have unlimited ability to take what you want from it in the expectation of ever-increasing good. Knowing this as truth in your heart and mind, you live in peace, having everything you could possibly imagine and more. You have everything you can dream of and much more.

Life smiles on everyone regardless of their perception. If it did not, you would not be alive. To understand wisdom, continually give thanks for your good while desiring more of it. It is natural to want to have more and to do better in life. You simply accept it as done. Music comes from all things including the clacking of beetles and the swoons of joy that lovers make. Art is in all places: No artist ever captured the supreme sunset or the supreme sunrise; no carver can make a tree.

Proceeding with your daily study, you will come to know no limits. At this moment you must continue in your devotion to your work. If you do not endeavor to proceed beyond what you already know, this moment is also a blocking point. If you accept the idea that you have accomplished all that you can because of this blocking point then you have learned nothing in all your years of study. The Spirit of the Thing Itself tells you that there is more to be had and so you must continue to ask of it to reveal ever more. And because you are sincere in your heart, it will. That is the nature of Heaven.

36

Unseen—the promise of the warrior is frightening

Unseen—the ideas of the scholar are frightening

Unseen—the works of the magician are frightening

Unseen—the words of the king are frightening

Unseen—the wit of the wise is frightening

Seen—the words of poets are foolish

Seen—the actions of braggarts are foolish

Seen—the thoughts of yourself are foolish

Know—it is deeds not words

When things are not seen for what they are, a man cannot understand what their original intent was supposed to be. Things and words become an extension of the person and therefore they lose meaning. As a result they lose value. If a man is of importance and comes to be unimportant, it is because he loses the perception of his own value. When it is regained he will ascend to a higher position than ever before if he so desires. Maintaining his shortcomings, he will sink ever lower.

Most men sink ever lower. They cannot understand that original authority comes from Heaven and, refusing to acknowledge it, they think they are their own creations. How foolish, how shallow, and how vain. To make a difference, a man should indulge himself in the aspects of godliness. Then he doesn't have to concern himself with his limited perspective.

If you think that, as a result of your training, you are ascending to an ever-higher plane, you are correct. But it is essential to understand that only because of Heaven's grace does it come to be. Strive harder, with more intelligence. Accepting your continued growth with grace and ease, acknowledge the beneficence of Heaven, the Spirit of the Thing Itself.

37

All things are without energy

All things are energy

Things do not have to be that which they already are

No importance in imposing your will

Tell people what they are to do

What will happen if they don't

They see for themselves or do not

Ever blaming you for their failures

Passion exists when a man sees his value

Not terrified of failure

He takes pleasure in his work

Not questioning his place in life

He sees all there is to see

He loves and is loved in return

The land exists in peace

Forces from without withhold

The driver protects the chariot

Things exist in their own totality. Only when incorrectly perceived do things appear to be incomplete. When you tell a man what to do, he will usually think he is considered unwise. This will anger him. If he is threatened, he will revolt and consider your directions faulty. He will blame you for his failures. Perception of unity with the Way shows no man knowing more than another—nor any less. It is required that each man teach another and that all men remain equal in nature. This is the Way.

Can you imagine how delightful things would be if everyone had what everyone else had? An individual would not strive after another's goods. Prosperity would explode throughout the cosmos without restriction. Everything could exist according to every man's desire. Heaven would cease being manipulated in consciousness and harmony would simply be. Your technique would be unrestricted and your passion would flow through your joy to your work.

To think that the Unnameable would permit outside forces to overcome its blessings is foolish. If no resistance to the outside force was established, Heaven would have no reason to intimidate the population. The wise king knows this and does not impose his will. Imposing his desires he will be forced to spend excessively to keep the realm constant. It will never be constant. Impending reversal of fortune accompanies forced integration. The land is always in turmoil.

38

Men of strength and love live in strength and love

Are sustained by strength and love

Not flashing it untowardly

Not boasting of accomplishment their actions speak

Not concerned with rewards of work

The work is the reward itself

Virtue is real when not expressed as such

Base men will use force if not obeyed

In time they will not be obeyed and will use the fist

In time the man's fist will fail

The Fist of God will prevail

Morality requires previous thought

It leads to etiquette

It leads to justice which is man ordained

It leads to anarchy which is people ordained

It leads back to Heaven which is God ordained

You can only be that which you think you are. When you try to be more or less than that you will find you are without peace and serenity. You will make distinctions between right and wrong as you perceive them and move yourself that much farther from the truth—which does not care.

The essence of being is such that there can be no distinction between what is right and wrong. If you seek to control others, you must first control yourself. But this is ancient wisdom and therefore suggests your loss of remembrance. If you try to impose your will, it is because you are afraid you are not at home and must use your fist to enforce your desire. This will rebound against you in turn. Then you will make rules and consider applications of those rules to those you favor, making a distinction against those you do not favor. And so it goes, ending nowhere but at the beginning, where all of man's desires must be redreamed. Except that the universe never begins and never ends. And still it does not care because it goes on forever.

What folly it is to think that you are capable of being on the same level as God. How much greater is the folly to think you are not. Accept yourself as the perfection of your own ideal and live your life accordingly, asking Heaven, not other men, for guidance.

The Living Tao

39

The Way is without duplication

Everything is composed of its many parts

Nothing is total without complement

Sky understands void

Earth understands sky

Man understands earth

Animals understand man

Flowers understand animals

The lower supports the higher

The higher realizes the lower

All things are in support of one another

But Heaven is All

The strength of the earth is in the soil

Jade tinkles gently in the breeze

Or it breaks

Whatever exists is made with all of the parts of everything else. The substance that creates the stars is the same substance that creates man. All things understand their relation to everything else in the natural and harmonious order of the Way. Only man, because of his arrogance, does not understand. When he does understand he is considered wise and lives a life of ecstasy.

When the chain of understanding is broken, chaos results and nothing functions in serenity. The highest ideal rests on the foundation of the base. How could it be otherwise? If things are to function from the top to the bottom, the bottom must support that which rests upon it. That is why kings do not have anything to govern without the people beneath them. If the king is virtuous, the people will support him. The strength of the nation is in the land and not in the frivolity of trinkets regardless of their presumed worth, which is determined by men concerned with earthly profit. You are the only one who can determine your worth. Base it on the value you give to other men for their worth. This is the Way.

40

Everything returns to its place of nothingness

In its speed and strength is its power and quickness

What is came from what is

And returns again to be reformed

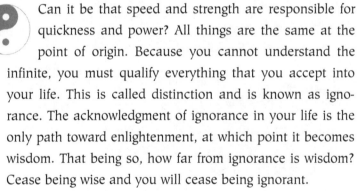 Can it be that speed and strength are responsible for quickness and power? All things are the same at the point of origin. Because you cannot understand the infinite, you must qualify everything that you accept into your life. This is called distinction and is known as ignorance. The acknowledgment of ignorance in your life is the only path toward enlightenment, at which point it becomes wisdom. That being so, how far from ignorance is wisdom? Cease being wise and you will cease being ignorant.

Power and quickness are the essential ingredients of learning to place value in the Infinite. It is for this reason that speed and strength are secondary to quickness and power in all forms of life. They are only external representations of the Infinite on the plane of the finite. Power and quickness are revealed as truth when man understands the need to return to the source of all things. The way to excel in understanding life is revealed to him who desires to know It.

41

A learned man hears of the Way and pursues It

A common man looks and puts it away

Foolish people hear and laugh at Its beauty

If people did not react the way they do

It would not be the Way

As above and so below

No difference in what it is

Some see bottom as top

Some see deep as shallow

Eternity is momentary

Great form has no shape

Great music is without sound

Great power is without presumption

No corners or edges in space

Time does not stand

It never moves

Space never is and time never was

That some men will acknowledge it or not is unimportant to the Thing Itself. The infinite is not concerned with what you think it is or should be. Though time-less-ness and space-less-ness must be real in the finite order for Eternal Being to exist, how can a finite man know that which is infinite? It is true that, if you know what exists, you also know that which does not exist, there being no change in the universe except for man's perceptions. If this were not so, the Unknowable would have been born and would, in time, die. This is not possible. The Eternal is always present everywhere—here, now. Time is important to man because he sees his body wither and die. The unknowing-ness frightens him and he seeks to dominate all other things, but this is incorrect perception. Aging prepares man to enter another level of existence, which cannot be identified through the finite.

Forget this wisdom and continue to practice your trade. It is God's self-identity through you, Heavenly thing that you are. Never be envious of another's lot in life. Without the butcher, the surgeon has nothing to eat. The wise surgeon knows this. He therefore becomes great and cuts with perfection while giving thanks that the butcher is skilled as well. The butcher, wise as well, cuts with precision and absolute perfection.

42

Life is an extension of one two three

Limitless and continuing to add

Itself becoming ever more

It is Heaven Earth and Man

In any order each becomes the other or none exist at all

The Sun shines in the warrior's face

Beating upon his back it is all the same

This is the balance of the Universe

That blessings are both glad and sad

Good and bad is required to explain It All

No difference except for where one stands

What works here does not work there

One begets what one begets

Or that man can teach me all there is

The universe continues to unfold through what we consider eternity. There can be no limit to its being-ness. Things can only be measured by thoughts of Heaven, fixtures on earth, and thoughts in the individual person. If we were not present, we would never be able to conjecture about anything.

Of same things there can be no difference except to see the other side of it. This is called a "point of view." In going and coming, there is only one direction that a warrior can take. Appreciating the sun in his face and then at his back he still feels the warmth. If you think your fortune is assured, you must know that another's is as well. You must therefore understand the need for charity and compassion toward all things. It is the same with what we perceive as blessings. There is always the difference in point of view that will enable a man to determine if a blessing is good or bad— but good or bad only for him. Without this understanding, you will certainly perish.

When you find a person who practices evil and is rewarded for his actions, understand that as Perfect Good as well. Do not expect another's life to unfold as your own. You are both the same in Heaven's eyes. If this is not so, the man who can explain otherwise is the true teacher and I will listen to him with all hearing.

43

Water penetrates the hardest stone

Fire boils the densest ice

Air corrodes the crystallized thing

Earth rots the firmest tree

All is no-thing in the face of the Eternal

To learn something you must leave it and come back

Eventually the truth will reveal itself

It is the Way of all things

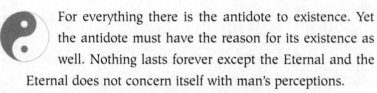 For everything there is the antidote to existence. Yet the antidote must have the reason for its existence as well. Nothing lasts forever except the Eternal and the Eternal does not concern itself with man's perceptions.

It is possible to penetrate the mysterious depths of the universe. There is also need to plumb common knowledge. It is based on the desire to know a higher truth. What you perceive to be the essence of a thing must be considered by your self. Constant study will reveal more of the matter as you proceed to enter the depths of the soul of the thing. When you find yourself unable to proceed in your studies it is time to forget them for a while and concentrate on another matter. This will give you the ability to release the tension of your own desire and permit the Spirit of the Thing Itself to penetrate into your consciousness. When you have cleared your mind of the disturbances that restrict you from your further advancement, you will come to know the newness of your thinking and see it manifest in your life.

This is the nature of the Spirit of the Thing Itself. It can be no other way. It must be free to express itself through you, in you, as you, and for you. Regardless of the obstinacy of the matter, sincerity of desire will eventually cause it to reveal itself. That is Its own gift to Itself, that It reveals Itself to him who truly desires to know.

When you practice your craft, be sure to understand the reason for your persistence. If anything is anything, everything is everything. There is no such thing as spirituality in one thing and not in another. How could that be? True desire to be more than you consider yourself to be will always cause the Spirit of the Thing Itself to be revealed in all things or nowhere ever. This is the Way of Heaven.

The mightiest warrior is nothing without the farmer to grow and the cook to prepare his food, an armorer to prepare his weapons, a teacher to guide him, a lover to soothe him, and Heaven to love him.

You are the Spirit of the Thing Itself. *That* is the Spirit of the Thing Itself.

44

What is most important
You or what you do

Which is worth more
You or Heaven

Which costs more
Gain or loss

The virtuous man
Values his work as much as himself
Values Heaven as much as himself

Seeing no difference between loss or gain
Having won a victory he strives to understand more
Having suffered defeat he strives to understand more
There is no difference except for himself
There is no difference except for the opinions of others

A man must be sure of himself and must understand his own value. If he does not, he is constantly under pressure to prove his worth to other men. Everyone will ask him to explain his behavior except Heaven. He can, in time, learn to discern the value in his own eyes and the perceptions of other men. That learning will show him the path back to the beginning. And so he begins, from a different point of view, to see the true point of view, that he and his work are one and the same. This pleases Heaven and the proper path to travel will be made clear. He comes to understand that he and Heaven are the same thing.

When a man must make decisions concerning his further growth, it is best that he retreat from the world of men and seek his own counsel. Knowing himself to be as the same substance as Heaven, he will soon realize where he is going and where he has gone astray. Everything he attempts to understand will be revealed in all its forms and he will know when to choose what he considers right and what he considers wrong. This is correct action of mind as both right and wrong are correct in the eyes of Heaven. That being so, truth will be revealed to him as he desires it to reveal itself.

If he becomes confused, he will simply say to himself that "of confusion and errors there are none and God simply is done." Denying the implications of morality according to the needs of other men, he will be free to choose his own destiny. Doing so, he will truly become one with the Way.

45

Blame the wise man for the world's ills

He tells you that competence rules the day

Heat is denied with no motion

Coldness is dealt with motion

The empty pitcher provides space for more

Work is never finished even if the worker dies

When a man dies his work first begins

Sages look like idiots

Idiots appear to be filled with wisdom

Such is the Way of the universe

It is constantly celeritous

Neither here nor there

None understand the Way

It is unknowable

STOP and GO

There is no such thing as knowing just as there is no such thing as unknowing. It is all nonetheless perfect whatever the ideal. The ideal is in your mind, or what you perceive as your mind. Words of wisdom sometimes make no sense and idiotic statements contain the truth of the ages. Nothing is happening except for what is happening. Right and wrong have no need to exist.

The king understands this and rules wisely—whatever that may mean. It is his work. No one knows the answer to anything that cannot be measured, and all that can be measured is only "things," which do not last in time. Time is constantly fleeting at the same time in all directions, even the eight unknown. Because it is mostly unknown, it is wise to stop forcing your intentions and to go on with your life in harmony with Heaven, accepting the ease and grace provided for all who recognize the Supreme Reality.

When a man decides that a particular road is the way for him to travel, it is because either Heaven or the man himself has chosen this path. It does not matter how his life comes to be. The only thing to be concerned with is the conscious realization that he is as one with the one. Fate and free will do not function on the cosmic plane. They intersect each other and provide the substance of life.

46

When the Way is understood

There is no need to fight for gain

Exquisite horses fertilize the fields

Warhorses pull carts filled with food

The Way is content with Itself

There are no exquisite horses

There are no horses for war

Ownership leads to loss

Unless one's mind is very strong

It leads to greater wanting

Greater wanting leads to stealing

Stealing leads to murder

Murder leads back to understanding the Way

Contentment is content with its own contentment

Exquisite horses pull the finest carriages. Warhorses pull the cannons of destruction. In the same way, when they are used for the benefit of man and give the pleasure of their nature they cease being used for things that can cause grief. It is best to be content with life. This does not mean that you are static in mind and body. It means that you value the value of your self and therefore are able to experience anything you desire. You will not fear anyone taking anything from you. You will have what you need and there will be no need to hoard.

When a man perceives that his work is more unusual than that of others, he becomes unable to see clearly the value of his labors to all of man. He becomes fearful that others may take part of his work and he chooses not to share it with others. He desires more than he had before and seeks to gain it through means other than Heaven's. This leads to erroneous thought patterns, including vices, which keep society from moving forward in peace and harmony.

It is the rare man who can understand that the work, once done, is for the benefit of all. Without this perception, the work becomes stagnant and does not do that for which it was originally intended. Envy and greed do nothing but stop the flow of Divine Right Action, creating the problems that man is faced with at all times.

The wise king understands this and rules without strain. When the people are happy, it will show in their work and in their lives. Knowing this, they will also understand that all things are created when required. And knowing this, there is no problem in all things ceasing to be when they are no longer required. How difficult it is to realize how unimportant you really are if you think only of yourself. That is the true value of importance. You cannot understand life if you have only created children. You must also create yourself. Being content, and being content with that contentment, will enable you to create newer and better things, enhancing your life and the lives of those around you.

47

It is not necessary to run outside to see things

It is not necessary to study matters to understand them

It does not require that you impose your will

The profound reality of the Universe

All things are all known to all men

Now

Never mind the more you seek the less you find

Never mind the more you desire the less you have

All is already yours

Accept it

Practice breeds familiarity

It is the true understanding of the Matter

There is no need to seek outside yourself for anything. Even the highest answers are revealed to the one who truly desires to know the truth. Once that information is known to you, simply act on it and delve deeper into its true meaning. The more you seek, the more you find. This is the reality of the universe, but it does not mean that it is the invincible way. *That* is unknowable.

Everything you could ever desire is already formed in your life once it is in your mind. But it must be in your mind. Otherwise it will not know you desire its existence. If you would only believe that you have at your command all of the universe, you would become comfortable knowing that your life manifests in truth as you desire it. When you understand this, you will cease wanting and, accordingly, have. The more you desire something, the more readily it will appear in your life. Constantly and consciously strive for it.

Do not concern yourself that you desire something with all of your self and it does not appear. Continue to desire and it must. It is compelled by its very nature. You simply have to accept it as so. Do not concern yourself that it appears in a form other than the one you desired. Simply reapproach your desire and correct your thinking.

48

By constant study a man learns

More of the thing he desires to know

He daily loses ignorance of the matter

Until at last he has lost his reason for learning

And becomes the thing itself

Letting go of all in time he comes to understand

That all is revealed and all is complete

He is then beyond the need to win or lose

When a man pursues the study of something, he must by the nature of space and time lose that which is being replaced or there will be no advancement. His ignorance of the matter is being replaced by knowledge of it. When all is accepted as known—and all *is* known—the Way is clear and truth reveals itself. The Spirit of the Thing Itself enjoys the student more than the student could ever enjoy the Thing Itself. However, both enjoyments must be the same. Fulfillment implies completion.

It is a man's use of his knowledge that makes his life complete. When knowledge is complete, more comes to be in his life than he ever conceived. When you practice certain techniques in your craft, and come to see that they are merely extensions of your own spirit, you will know what this means. When you decide that you already do understand what this means, you can apply it to your craft. Then it becomes you and never has to be revealed.

49

Free in mind there is no need to compare

You know love only if you know hate

It is better to know neither

Do not make judgments that you cannot understand

And continue to live in the Way

Death is a meaningless event

It merely takes you to the next self-defined place

Which is not correct

You can only know what you do not know

By knowing It

The wise man's sayings do not preclude the ability of an idiot to know the truth also. It should be realized that perception is only another way to be. How could it be otherwise? Is one man smarter or wiser than another? Even with material things, my wealth will never be surpassed by yours unless I covet yours. Yours should never be less than mine.

The only true way to understand something is actually to experience it. The reality of death can only be known through experience. Until it is actually known and can be articulated, it is only speculation. Why concern yourself with death when you can better spend your time living to the fullest?

Knowing this, a man lives his life fully and does not want things that would increase his concern for possession. He simply increases his lot in life by direct choice. When death comes, he meets it with a peaceful heart—without pain or suffering—and he is lifted to the next protocol.

50

Thirteen entrances and exits

Make man vulnerable when he lives in the world

Four limbs and nine cavities

Comprise the living body

Grossness of being keeps a man from the Way

In ignorance he thinks these things maintain his life

They are only devices

Only devices doing nothing to enhance reality

The man of wisdom lives in the Eternal

Permits nothing evil to enter his body

Nothing evil to enter his mind

Nothing evil to enter his life

Kept free of poison

Kept free of disease

Kept free of pain

Kept free of old age

By contemplation of the Divine Ideal

He loves because it is his nature

Invulnerable to death it too is his nature

Lions do not eat him buffaloes do not gore him

Weapons do not touch him

They have no target

He enjoys a glass of water

Even if it is not wine

The openings of the body must be kept clear and clean. The muscles and the sinews of the body must be kept in good repair. Ignorance of these matters permits easy access to disease. Having nothing to do with life or death, the wise man understands that the body is merely an instrument to carry him through his limited days. Maintaining perfection of being by knowing the truth of the universe as the divine expression of the divine ideal, he sees external threats flee from his presence. They will seek easier targets. A wise man's death is a laughing matter. Much more so than all the pleasures of life—anyone he would seek on the physical plane, sexual pleasures notwithstanding, or delicious food, or the joy of his labors.

When he becomes totally conscious of the mind and the body, the unimportance of immortality becomes evident.

He is free from the worry of disease and its attendant vexations and stays that way. Being aware of his presence in the world and keeping his own counsel, he does not fear the eventuality of death and becomes invulnerable to it. He enjoys all there is to enjoy. A glass of water is as delicious as a glass of wine, though they are different in appearance and taste. It is a matter of taste. It is a matter of choice.

Without knowing the truth of one's own art, it is difficult to understand another's. When acceptance of the self is understood, there is no problem seeing the value of another man's work. If it is done well, it is recognized as such. If it is done with callousness, that is recognized as well.

51

You have been given life

Not by your parents

There is reason for you to be here

Wherever here is

Whatever reason is

You perceive it for yourself

All things are obedient to the Infinite

If they are not then you are not here

Do not seek to command seek to teach

Do not seek to obey seek to understand

Make use of your eyes or lose them

Make use of your ears or lose them

Make use of your mind or lose it

Give life to things but don't seek to own them

Give death to things but don't seek to own them

You are part of the entire cosmos even if you do desire to be so. Even if you do not. Your mind works with you or without you. It doesn't care one way or another. The mystic power of the universe is that It is not concerned that It is. Only by permitting man to be part of Its ideal can It come to know more of Itself. There is no such thing as mystic power.

Being here suggests that you are only present in the finite. Being here suggests that you are conscious of your world and its surroundings. When you are in such a state of being, very little can interfere with your personal advancement into the depths of your chosen art.

Seek to teach only that which you truly know by experience. To do otherwise means that you are speculating and passing wrong information to your student. This only leads you farther away from your true being. Likewise, seeking to obey because of the possible rewards restricts you from further growth. It is understanding that frees you from your self-imposed limitations. Your actions are the actions of Heaven and without your mind to guide them you will never be fulfilled.

52

Universal Mother created the world

Her own reasons

The Mother had children

Sons who would never understand Her

Though stay close She will nourish and protect you

She is the source of all

Stop your senses and accept the perfection She offers

Stay busy with contemplation of Her Divine Ideal

Permit Her to do the work and reap the rewards

See small things and appreciate the large

Little by little become the totality of Her

She reveals all that needs to be known

Let your Knowingness continue to grow

 There is no need to strive for perfection, you already have that. The Universal Mother holds nothing back from Her children. It is the children who resist Her perfection because they insist on knowing Her reasons for being. It does not matter that you see the universe as His or Hers or Its. That is your choice. It is, however, the desire of the Spirit of the Thing Itself to give pleasure by being more of Itself through you as part of your recognition. That is why it is meaningless to force something into being by means of willpower. If you wish to change conditions, do so by thinking the best thoughts for your experience.

Being the causation of all things, the Mother is also the Father creating Its own desire. Stop your senses from interfering with your perceptions. Desire to know more of the particular thing and the particular thing will always reveal more of itself, until by your own nature you increase your ability to know ever more. There is nothing mysterious in this thinking.

It is the same with the accumulation of wealth and other material abundance. The more you have of something, the more you should want of it to express yourself more fully. But it is done more easily with acknowledgment of the source of all things and not with the hidden desire to wrest that which belongs to others away from them. Forcing desire is also a waste of time and energy. The expression of all protects its vehicle. It makes no sense to worry about losing it. You can't. Its already you—who you are, where you are, what you are. There is nothing to attain.

If you are critical of details, remember to see the overall picture as well. If you do not, you will miss everything completely. Strive to be one with knowingness. It is the truth of the matter.

53

Who has more than I

The insecure man asks always

Though staying on the path

Having nothing I have all

Royalty suggests arrogance

Fields are overgrown with weeds

Kings care not that granaries are empty

Sharpened swords at their sides

Silken robes on their bodies

Fine carriages and magnificent steeds

They glut themselves while thieves run rampant

How can you possibly be content with your lot in life if you are not aware of your lot in life? Your lot in life is not based on that of others. It is based on your acceptance of yourself as the divine receiver of all that is good in the universe. This is especially true when you are seeking to raise your consciousness to a new, higher level. Having this mentality, you are not concerned that you have or you do not have. By simple acceptance of it as your own, everything that is needed is there for you. Regardless of your apparent position in life, do not take your present condition as constant. To do so is to accept defeat before you have entered the battle. Stop desiring to become less than you are by thinking of what you are not. What you perceive yourself to be has nothing to do with what others perceive you to be.

Eventually royalty will suffer its own devices by not caring about its sources of supply. Showing off their finery causes others who lack finery to think unjust thoughts. The people will try to determine how they can attain those fine things, not caring how they are acquired. What has that to do with you? Nothing. Do not be jealous of what another man thinks he owns. It is your responsibility alone to enjoy all the finery of life available to you. This includes becoming the king. But remember, if you do become the king, with the new position you will acquire kingly problems.

Ascend to your heart's desire and be glad that you are able to do so without stress or strain. Then, when you are truly there, the imaginary problems will cease to exist because it is your nature to be where you are.

54

The true foundation is Eternal

It can never change

It is all change

Stay firm in It and nothing will affect you

Leave the path and you stray into chaos

Cultivate the path in your heart your soul shall stay true

Cultivate the home riches will overwhelm you

Cultivate the mind genius will run rampant

Cultivate the world you will know the Universe

Your beingness being all

Men will know you as such

The warrior understands the need to grasp the funda-
mentals. He does this by constantly practicing them
until they are a reaction from his heart. In such a manner, his blade appears without seeming to have been drawn.
It appears by means of the Spirit of the Thing Itself in the

soul of the warrior. He also knows that to change a technique just for the physical appearance is a way to approach death without dignity.

As you develop more insight into the Way you have chosen, difficulties will disappear and knowledge will give way to understanding. Being beyond commonplace thoughts, you will go along your path unseen. When you desire to love, you will love completely, and when it is time to go to war you will do so with the same passion.

What do you care about the thoughts of others? Can you think you are less important than others? Can you think you are more important than others? Who is anyone to think they are right or wrong about anything except what is considered acceptable in their society? No one is capable of judging a man who does not judge others. A belief in false rumors can beguile your serenity.

It is best to maintain rigorous training and to reap the rewards than it is to permit others to influence your thinking. Most influencers are afraid of their own shadows and will presume to tell you what is best for you because they cannot make decisions for themselves. You must know and believe that you are the only one who exists in the universe. The more you can accept this, the more you can accept all the others—and wish them well.

How do I know this? Because I know this.

55

Stay childlike and be one with Heaven

Without seeking gain all is given

Snakes will not bite and eagles will not pluck your eyes

Though bones become brittle and sinews weaken

Spirit is forever robust

To wonder at the fullness of it all

Continue to give pleasure when not all is known

Children learn that all is different

Enjoying each and every thing

Sameness in all things abounds

The Way is maintained in peace

Deny the Way and you will die strangely

 If a man sees life through a child's eyes, he sees the wonder of all things and does not select one thing over another. In time, he lives with complete ease and freedom. When he begins to make distinctions he loses the perfection of the Way and his identity is incorrectly perceived. Even the variations of supposed evil in the world evade the man of conscious wisdom. He does not deal with matters that do not concern him, for he knows that if he does, he will die in a peculiar manner.

When attacking a problem in life, it is best to see yourself as the reason for the problem's existence. Then, should you desire to do so, easily change the conditions in your life by correct thinking. The results will be astounding. All will be granted to you in peace and you will not strive after false dreams.

56

Screaming and shouting they do not know
In silence wisdom makes itself bluntly evident

He does those things that make him one
With his fellows he is lost in them
If he does not comply
They will break his heart

He who is able to maintain perfection
Knowing and not knowing
Has mastered the entire world

Balance comes from experience
But not all experience shows the Way
Things should be thought through deeply
Or not at all

 Once a man understands the difference between knowing and not knowing, he is able to reach out and teach
those who would seek to understand the Infinite. Truly

knowing something makes a man desire not to talk of it in public. Realizing this, he will not be under constant ridicule by those less learned. In this manner he becomes the loudest of all by his silence. His actions speak for themselves and he continues on the path for his own enjoyment.

By doing things that are required by a group, he may hope to attain freedom but will soon learn that his own mind is not his own. This is because he will structure his behavior according to the needs of the group. When he finally frees himself, they will seek revenge and attempt to thwart his ideal.

Knowing that all things are evidence of their own being, he understands the importance of seeing both sides of a matter. Experience may not always be the best teacher unless a man seeks to understand his own motivations. This learning should reveal more of itself each time it is considered. Still, experience does not always reveal the truth of the matter being sought. A man should continue to think matters through even if the results are what was expected. In such a way, better work is produced each time it is attempted. Not to do this restricts the perfection of the work from radiating its glory and is a fatal error in judgment.

57

Ordinary men try to govern men

Creating extraordinary problems when they don't concur

The best action is no action

Stay in the Way

Action followed by action creates inhibition

Law after law creates thieves and murderers

Weapons continue to create war

Business after business creates waste

But the Way is without doubt

A sensible man does not meddle in the ways of the world

Not giving orders he does not preach

Constantly examining himself

His words may sound like madness

His Way appears strange and he appears to be alone

Sensible yet knowing how to protect himself

Using the Way to attain his desires

The Way will not permit him to be sad

When a man stops trying to take control of things that have nothing to do with him he can ascend to the heights of beauty and knowledge. He realizes the foolishness of trying to control others when he is trying to attain his own perfection. Not realizing the absurdity of his desire to control other men, he forgets his studies and begins to question the Intelligence of the Universe. When It reveals things to him that may frighten him, he thinks with profound good reasoning and the Way truly loves him.

During interaction with other men he sometimes becomes befuddled until he takes himself away from the crowd and concentrates on his own work. This is extremely hard to do and even the mightiest warriors have fallen prey to the inadequacies of their own intelligence. There will always be times when the loneliness of ascension will cause him to fear his own development. It is frightening to be alone and without companionship. When he comes under public scrutiny they will listen to his words and think he is mad because he is talking of the universality of all things and truly believes he is one with all men by his individuality. As the Way truly loves him, he takes solace in knowing that he is proceeding to higher levels of consciousness and his aloneness does not give him grief. In this way he is in the world without self-doubt and is one with all men. Knowing he is not of the world, he acknowledges Heaven and this gives him joy. He cannot speak an untruth.

To reach this level of understanding of his true self is costly in terms of being constantly misunderstood, until with true understanding he is free of his opinion of others.

58

The more you govern the more nervous your people are

The less you govern the more they will seek to please you

The more a leader tells of his exploits

The more quickly do the people become bored

Do not be deceived

By the appearance of the enemy's armor

What looks mighty can be weak and the reverse as well

Good fortune can be quelled by bad behavior

Bad behavior can sometimes be virtuous

Do not determine which mask to wear

Instead wear none and be open to all

Even your enemies will love you

They will see they have nothing to fear

Their hatred will subside

Don't confuse with ideas that emulate cow dung

Don't amaze with ideas that emulate wisdom

The best way to be is not to be. No matter what you desire to attain or accomplish, it is best to pursue your goal. Everything you desire will come to be. It is not necessary to terrorize others. It is not necessary to awe or amaze them. They do that for themselves by not understanding your intentions if you have none other than living by the Way. There will be times when your best intentions will be misunderstood and you will have cause to regret your day. Overcome this by realizing your own fallacies and proceed to raise your consciousness to where you know and believe it should be.

You must be sure to keep your own counsel. When you try to explain a truth to those who are unable to identify with you, it causes them to think you are speaking one way and acting in another. When you have done something that you determine displeases you, you must begin to correct your thinking to correct the course of your Way. If you do not do this and disregard your inner feelings toward an action you have taken, you will surely fall into despair and, losing the Way, you will be hard-pressed to realign yourself with the realm of Heaven.

59

Serve God or rule man

You cannot do both

Though they seem the same

Using the Power of Heaven

Experience All the good

If you give man directions you may be in error

When God directs It is never in error

Know your position and understand the Mother

She will nurture you forever

Even including the Way for you to govern men

When a man seeks to understand the universe, many things are revealed that are normally hidden from view. The Cosmic Mother has no desire other than to give suck to Her children with all the joy and prosperity of Her consciousness. By ruling, kings are sometimes in error; this usually leads to the downfall of their empires; proper planning and thinking about the future were not conceived for the benefit of all. Kings, when selfishly motivated, are incorrect in their thinking even though it is correct for them to think they are.

Thinking before acting will permit the proper expression of the Spirit of the Thing Itself because you will have asked for guidance from Heaven. Then there can be no error. It will be the will of Heaven brought to demonstration by your adoration of the truth.

60

When governing the country

Look down from above by being level-headed

When frying small fish the less touched the better the taste

Quicker is the meal made ready

People do the best they can

Not thinking of ghosts of the past

They will desire to please the ruler

They will do what they have to do

Pleased with their own work

The more the Way is permitted to be Itself, the more easily the people will attain their desires. They will think less about the superstitions that may have frightened their ancestors. As ruler, you should see from above that it is so below. To be level-headed is to be in accord with your own desires expressed through the work of your people. They need not fear a sudden change in your temperament. Not being concerned with right or wrong, they are more likely to concentrate on their output without fear of disturbing the ruler. The ruler knows that if he tells his governors what he wants and they proceed to treat the people fairly, all will be done according to the Way and there will be no need for sacrifice.

In like manner, when you practice to become more at one with the Spirit of the Thing Itself, you will find a higher understanding of yourself in relation to It. You will see that all is one and there is no need to consider variation. Variation comes anyway. It is an expression of the will of Heaven.

The wise ruler understands that by constantly seeking the reason for his own motivations he will attain peace of mind. Growing is a painful process and sometimes inappropriate behavior reveals errors in your thinking. You should understand that this inappropriate behavior, when recognized as such, can then be redirected. It is free to express itself through changes in your perception of the Way.

61

Things flow from top to bottom

This is the Nature of things flowing

Sometimes they flow from bottom to top

Rivers fill the places between the land

Fish fill the rivers

Riverboats are filled with fish

This is the Way of Heaven

The larger the river the more fish

Becoming an ocean

It is filled with more boats

There are more fish to feed the people

Thanking Heaven for their bounty

Heaven continues to fill the rivers with fish

But no river can be the ocean

It is essential to understand that infinite supply comes from Heaven. If man continues to take without thanking the Source of all by acknowledging Its bounty, Heaven will still continue to fill the rivers and oceans. Man will continue to destroy his environment with his filth and when fish appear to cease being he will complain to Heaven.

When man destroys the rivers, he will think Heaven does not exist because he no longer has any fish to eat. He will create devious ways to take for himself that which was freely given to all. This will lead him farther from Heaven and he will destroy himself, but Heaven will never cease to exist. Everything derives from the Mother. If you do not think so, then where did you come from?

By carefully practicing your chosen discipline, the infinite supply of all things becomes evident. By constantly focusing on the goal you have set for yourself and by applying your work to that specific result, many profound things will be revealed to you in other areas of your life as well. Your life will be enhanced. No matter how you think a certain thing should appear, that thing will never be more than what it is and therefore can never be less either. What occurs by Divine Right Action is what man should strive to accept for himself. Attaining it, man calls this "perfection of being." He is still individualized as an extension of Heaven and will never be all things in his finite condition. He should be himself and not worry about being all things to all men.

62

The mystery of the Way unfolds
The good man his wealth
The evil man his riches

Words of wisdom are ever for sale
Manners are taken on the surface
Nothing to do with good or evil

When the emperor is crowned
His ministers are both good and evil
According to their needs
There is no right way to judge
There is no wrong way to judge

It is best for the king to understand stillness of integrity
Let the wise men work their craft
Let the evil men be forgiven
In this way the Way will prevail

Because it includes the judge's alleged virtue, judgment is never virtuous. A man is rich and has wealth whether he is good or evil. There is no way to tell how his conduct enabled him to attain his position. Men are filled with words that express the highest ideal and only they can understand their own minds according to their own needs. Unless you are perfect you cannot judge because your own vision is clouded by your own self-importance. If he is wise, the king will permit his ministers free reign in governing the country but he will carefully observe that they are not overstepping their bounds, causing the people to be unhappy. Through silence and knowing, the Way will unfold according to the desires of all concerned.

Manners are taken to be correct conduct by the ruling class as they themselves set the conventions of each rule. Rulers do not consider the needs of the working class. Each class behaves as it should, relative to its environment. What is good in one country may not be good in another and may even be considered evil. This is why it is best to maintain your own appropriate conduct without imposing yourself on another.

By letting wise men continue in their work, a balance of virtues develops between good and evil. But forgiving men the evil they have done does not mean their conduct in society is overlooked nor does it mean their actions are condoned. If a man has done a grievous wrong according to the needs of the entire group, that wrong must be reckoned with or the entire society will fall apart. Punishment must be meted out where it is required. Even if it is not, the true Way will still prevail.

63

It is best to be calm when working

Permit nothing to enter your thoughts except excellence

Taste gently without gluttony

The small parts maintain the large

When troubles are small

They are easy to control and divert

When they are large it is necessary to bring in the troops

The conflict continues to grow and is not easily quelled

A wise man would therefore do nothing in his life

But partake of the Glory of the Infinite

The Infinite is pleased

To offer everything he could ever desire

Never making promises too easy to keep

Knowing laxity will cause shame

He thinks before he acts

It is best to think in terms of accomplishment without thinking about how to accomplish the deed. Let the Spirit of the Thing Itself express its own-ness. The Infinite Mind knows more than man ever could and will therefore show the Way by Its own joy. The wise man knows that to ordain something means to accept it as done.

When there is a rumbling of conflict, the wise man knows that it is best stopped before it becomes a major problem. Without thinking arrogantly he considers the cause of the strife and quells it without showing force. Asking for guidance from Heaven, he knows that the answer is already given and accepting it as so, stands back. Doing nothing, he sees the result take place. He sees it done as he desires with the harmony by which the world was created.

How hard is this to understand? Simply ask for guidance from Heaven and know that it is forthcoming without restriction. This involves the faith *of* Heaven in man more than a man's faith in Heaven. It is absolute and true self-knowing. It is done through conscious acceptance of the ideal.

When a man promises to do something without having given thought to his words, he will find difficulty in fulfilling the goal. If he seeks to avoid his promise, he will fall into shame based on the thoughts of other men as well as his own shame if he does not consider his words prior to his actions.

64

Hold a sparrow in your hand before it becomes tame

Nurture your garden before the weeds run amok

Taste fresh berries before they are picked

Act without action and the future can be foreseen

Foreseeing the future you can know the result of labors

You can know the care to give to the project

You can understand the value of the work

Approach labor that is easy to fulfill

Not when problems of dis-ease must be dealt with

Take care to sense surroundings without bragging

Gains are lost before the beginning

Never place value on things hard to get

Never place getting on things of no value

Know the difference

By understanding the value of the work at hand you can easily approach your goal as you approached the idea in the beginning because you have seen the desired result in your mind. Once you have done that you can easily proceed, making changes in your consciousness as you go along. You can watch in amazement as the universe unfolds before you producing exactly that which you desire.

Work should not be labor, though your job should be effortless in maintaining perfection of thought. Do not dare to will the final result. Such action will interfere with the perfect expression of the ideal. Although it will still be exactly as you wish, the results will be shoddy and of poor quality. Even if it produces wealth, you will still be thought of in a dark fashion by those upon whom you have imposed your will through your sloth of mind. Do the work and let the goals appear as their own result.

All of your desires are easy for Heaven to fulfill. Never desire that which cannot be readily understood by your own mind. When an idea is revealed to you it should be kept to yourself so as to keep meddlers out of your mind.

65

Ancients did not instruct in wisdom

They did not enlighten by their word

They did not know they were enlightened

They did not know they were ignorant

Kings came and taught right and wrong

People became confused and thieves came forth

Making the masters continually change the rules

To maintain control

They should never have had to change

It is much easier to rule by not

And simply suggest what is desired

In the old days men did not define the correct method to behave in a certain circumstance. They simply proceeded to be one with themselves and produced things that enabled ease and comfort for themselves and others. It was not necessary for wise men to tell others how to behave.

There were no enlightened men because all men were unaware of enlightenment.

When men began to take charge of other men they had to permit certain of the common folk to be part of the plan. This was the second mistake. The first was that they decided to be in charge at all. Once the machinery of government was revealed, rulers' regulations had to be enforced to maintain control. This was called "protocol" and it only worked when everyone was in compliance. When the common man saw that he would be controlled against his will and that he could not focus on the Way, he became surly and did not cooperate with his heart. The ruler became angry, which caused him to impose more rules and further lead the people from the Way. Chaos resulted.

Do not rule men. They do not need to be ruled if you gently request of them what you desire. It is important for them to prepare food and build shelters for their families. Then they can do what is necessary for their practice and study of the Way. In this manner all things come to all people and no one wants for anything. An astute mind understands this very simple truth. Different tongues do not have to be revealed. There are no secrets kept from Heaven. There are no secrets to reveal.

66

Reality and appearance are both the Way

The wise man understands not to rule

Standing ahead to protect his children

He does not offer direction

He clears the way to the Way

He does not talk down instead he lifts up

True unconcern for their direction

He only offers his knowing

A man lives his life as he sees fit. If he is unhappy, he changes his mind. Unless he is a fool, he accepts things without understanding his ability to change circumstance. Standing ahead of his children, he sees himself as his own son. Being his own son, he is able to ask the father of himself for guidance to proceed accordingly.

It is not important for the king to think that his ideas are the best for the people. If he is truly concerned for them he will show it by permitting them to express themselves in the manner they wish. It will be for the betterment of all concerned. His guidance ensures that they will not hurt them-selves. This protection is given as a father to a son in that he guides the morality of the child but not the direction of the child's life. This king is truly wise. His children do not see him interfering and each is in total control.

When teaching a man about the Way, it is best to show him what good can come from it if he lets it be his life. In this way the man will be able to decide for himself what is to be done and what is to be had.

67

Does my Way of life appear that of a simpleton
Is my calmness and surety something that you fear
Will you control me with your machines

Machines in time comply with my desires
All things seek newer being-ness

My world is of compassion
Wasting not I want not
With no desire to be the chief

Compassion compassion
That Way love thyself
As the Infinite loves you

Those who think they are capable of seeing life for
themselves are right, though they may look like idiots
because they do not comply with the ways of the
world. Because they do not seek to control others, they
appear to be simple. They are not simpletons. They would
rather permit themselves to be calm with understanding of

purpose. This frightens men who desire to control and they will seek to avenge themselves because they do not see the Way for themselves. Seeking release from their fears, they continue to impose their wills on others who are at peace with Heaven. Imposers and the weak minded cannot stand to allow others to be free and so, regardless of how they establish control, they must fight to wield it. The wise man does not care what the imposer thinks and permits that man to do what he wants without concern. If the imposer becomes too aggressive, the people rise up and destroy him.

With or without compassion, in time all things fall apart to be reformed. There is a simple truth to understanding the Way. It is knowing that you are treating your world as you prefer it to treat you. When men of great wealth come to understand that which is the true value of life, they begin to give all of their possessions back to the people. It is called charity. But it should be charity with understanding. When such men die, the way they lived is their legacy to their children. Nothing becomes wasted.

Men who seek to take without giving interfere with the gifts of Heaven. The compassion of the generous, if it stops, will give rise to the greed and envy of those who would take without having given anything for it in return. If a man thinks in terms of universal compassion, he never wants for anything and always has enough for his fellow man. This is wisdom and it is the wise man who understands that it is folly merely to give without expecting benefit for himself. The Way is unconcerned with folly. It is man's responsibility to endeavor to do his work with joy and compassion.

68

Skilled in warfare I am not violent

Able to kill with one stroke I do not vent rage

Knowing the Power of the Way I do not enter conflict

Shunning arrogance conceit and false pride

Say I am virtuous

Say I am cowardly

Say I am God

Say I am a man of wisdom

You can never know what is in my mind

You can never know what is in my heart

If I am skilled in my craft I do not force my intentions on another by bragging. I will show another the Way if asked, but there is never a time when another man can understand the things I feel in my heart. You may be sympathetic to my cause but you can never be me, so any attempt to be so is folly on your part. I would be the bigger fool if I wanted you to follow my Way. I can only tell you what I know and the rest you must find out for yourself. There is no such thing as greater or lesser love or pain or hate or envy or understanding or awareness or anything one person has more of than another.

There is, however, a level of awareness that comes only when a man seeks, for himself, that which is unknown and is revealed according to his true desire by his consciousness of the Spirit of the Thing Itself. The Way does not care. The Way is your mind. The balance of the universe is also the Way. That is what a man should seek regardless of the discipline he chooses for his personal identification.

69

Not to invite the fight but to be it

Stand back and observe rather than plunge in without seeing

Not liking the odds I retreat

Not wasting my spirit I do not wave my sword

Drawn without leaving the scabbard

I am armed without weapons

The wise enemy does not attack

The foolish enemy considers the wise

It is not always wise to evade conflict nor is it possible unless there is constancy of purpose and consciousness. Man's life should not be based on his desire to move into another's territory. Such a man should be stopped by the valiant and worthy. Not to stop him invites disaster.

A strong presence indicates a man's strong resolve to understand the need for conflict, even in the pursuance of the Way. It also indicates an ability to do battle, knowing that ultimate victory is his regardless of the outcome. This is also the Way. The Way is not cowardly. The Way is not brave. The Way is only the Way and it is defined by the man pursuing his own truth for himself.

Why would someone want to enter into conflict without first knowing as many of its aspects as he can? If he does such a thing, he wields his sword with foolishness. When he waves his sword, he tells the enemy what they can expect if they should desire to attack. It is best to be still and observe all things as they are and then to know that his preparation is a drawn sword even though it is yet in its scabbard.

Wise men understand the foolishness of unnecessary combat. Fools, generally, are saved by those who know.

70

It is simple to follow the Way

Though few will try

Something with such ease can have no value

Not having come from someone in authority

They laugh at my attempt to be one with the Way

Fearing the unknown they do not come to terms with It

They fear their own truth

Let go of the self

The most difficult of easy things to do

Do not wear proud garments

If you are unable to appreciate their worth

It is easy to be one with the Way. That is why it is always difficult for men who are only in the world. Constantly expecting someone to define the way and conditions for them to live, they seek permission for their own existence knowing they live a lie. They will always attempt to prove to themselves and others that they are thinking for themselves.

Words and doctrines do nothing but interfere with the reality of a man's life. That a man must be true to his own mind before he can pay heed to others' minds is essential to understand. To take profit without giving back indicates meanness of spirit and will cause a man to fall. To elevate yourself beyond the realm of the material world will release your hold on all things. Then observe as the things of value do not release you. Such is love's Way.

Fearing to let go of things shows that you do not believe you truly have them. If you love something and you let it have its freedom, it will fly from you. If the thing you love loves you in return, it will never leave. Such is the meaning of proud garments.

71

Knowing little you control much information

Having much information you have little knowledge

Sickness is a state of mind

To cure it never have it

Become perfect by denying diseased thoughts

Symptoms do not have authority in this man's mind

They do not approach his body

You are sick or you are healthy according to your perception of your health. I would prefer to walk in perfect harmony with the Way knowing that divine health expresses itself through me and so I am never subject to the conditions of disease. I deny the authority of disease in my life and, knowing this as my truth, the symptoms are not permitted purchase in my heart, my mind, or my life.

It is simple to deny something its authority before it has the chance to take control of your life. It is called honoring the body. It is called honoring God. It is not wanting to be sick and doing what is necessary to maintain the perfection of being in physical and mental health. It is all perceived through your thoughts about your own body.

If a condition exists prior to your disavowing it, you must first decide to rid yourself of the idea that it exists in your life. You do this by accepting perfect health as the alternative. Then, slowly, your condition changes—but only as you believe it does.

72

To defy authority is not the Way

Duress and civil disobedience make prison walls

Never containing the malice that impropriety breeds

Know yourself and not show yourself

The first step toward virtue

It matters what you say in private

It matters what you do in public

To you

Do not permit those in authority to rule without just cause

Defy them by noncompliance

Think well of yourself

Let that be your answer

There is no way that the entire population can accept the rule of the ruling class, especially when inequality is the structure of the day. But to revolt openly shows lack of ability to wrest control in the most intelligent and logical manner. Noncompliance will bring down the walls of the government when the government is unable to keep the people happy. This takes less time and effort than it does to break down the fortress and rebuild it. By your silence the walls crumble much more quickly. This is hard to understand because rabble-rousers are under the impression that violence begets calm. The unlearned among the people think in that manner as well. It is the ignorant trying to lead the unknowing. By permitting the people to live their own lives, the wise ruler maintains control over the people.

Difficulties arise when there are different rules for different groups of people. Even though it would appear that there is compliance by all the people, if he is aware of the conditions of his state, the ruler will see that turmoil can rise up at any time. Playing favorites, he must know that in time there will be discord that will lead to chaos even though things appear to be calm. By their very nature people will revolt and create disharmony among themselves. This does not bode well for the ruler who must then maintain authority through applications of fear. When that happens, all of the people will devise conditions that maintain them in favorable light. They will do this by making the ruler think they are complying while, in truth, they will be planning his demise.

73

A man who defies the Heavens will kill

A man who does not defy the Heavens will kill

Neither is right or wrong

Heaven does not care either way

Heaven does what you will

Heaven complies with your desire

Heaven does not know you are doing anything

Heaven does not care if you do or you do not

The master plan unfolds according

To a man's knowing himself

It unfolds according to a man's desire

To live in harmony or not

Nothing more and nothing less

Yin and yang are the opposites of each other and indicate that there are two sides to every condition. Though there may be no such thing as yin and yang, it is not to suggest that they do not exist. Everything is in the mind of the beholder and what is perceived by one man as right or as wrong is likewise perceived by another as the reverse. Heaven does not care one way or the other. Heaven is only interested in being interested in itself—yin and yang notwithstanding.

By knowing that you are the extension of Heaven, you can easily come to enjoy and experience all that you truly desire. This is the true Way of Heaven. While the universe continues to unfold in its direction, it continues to have more and more of Itself. There is no limitation to the growth of the universe and there is no limitation to the growth of a man if his heart is directed toward his own truth.

74

Unafraid to die

No value in threatening death

You cannot know what he thinks

Unafraid to be

He is more than what he thought

Fools would assume to do what he does

The executioner is a master at chopping heads

It is his Way to please Heaven

Those who would seek to do the same

Find they have chopped off their hands

All people know that, in time, they will perish. If you think you can control them with a threat of death you will be amazed that they do not care at all and will continue to misbehave. When the king tells the people that he needs more executioners, the people will be frightened and think perhaps their turn to be executed is coming. They will revolt and the revolt will be against the king. Some will think that by becoming executioners themselves they can save their lives by appearing to approve of the king's edict.

Execution does not stop crime. Shame does. The Way shows the way. When men are considered evil by those who express evil themselves, a turmoil comes to exist in the land. Men will do whatever they think they can and will have their share. Then, in his fear of losing control of the land, the king will issue more and more death warrants. And it continues to go and go in the same manner until there is complete chaos and lack of civility among all men.

A wise man teaches his son the correct behavior to receive the allness of Heaven. If the son does not know these things it is because his parents did not teach him. Perhaps it is because the parent's parents did not teach them either. Heaven eventually reveals to each man the truth of being. When this is accepted, all things become harmonious. Until then, there is chaos, which results in men cheating each other and finally in men killing each other in the name of self-supposed justice.

The Spirit of the Thing Itself can only reveal of itself what it is requested to reveal of itself. If madness rules, then the Spirit of the Thing Itself has no opinion. It will still express its joy.

75

Too much is taken from the people
More than necessary to run the government
The people will become hard to rule
They will learn to steal

If the fruits of their labors are freely given
To those who are undeserving
The people will see this as interference in their lives
Becoming unafraid
They will learn to steal

The man who does not work to fill his belly
Screams at the lack of food
He has learned to steal
And has been graced to do so

 A wise king will only take from his people that which he honestly needs to maintain the country. In this manner he strengthens his people. There will always be work for the just and the just will always work. Loafers will see that there is not enough for them to steal and they will have to produce or they will die. They will come to understand that the best part of taking from society is giving to it so it can be enjoyed by their children.

A wise ruler will never take from the productive area of his realm and pour it into the nonproductive area. The people who are not productive will always complain that they are not being given enough and will create more reason for the king to give them additional food. It will never be enough. If the ruler is just, the workers will give generously, knowing they are being provided for by the king and are not being taken advantage of. The people will love and respect him and he will have more than he ever could have gotten by himself.

76

In the beginning man is soft and tender

In old age bones become hard and brittle

Everything lives and everything dies

It is virtuous to know when to bend

When to stay firm

When to keep resolve

Strong and mighty topple to the ground

Soft and yielding rise to Heaven

When a child cries, even with gusto, it is still gentle and asking. The mother sees to it that the baby is fed. And so it is with Heaven when delivering that which is asked of it. Learning the lessons of life or perishing, the child soon learns that arrogance and stubbornness avail him nothing. Without knowing the ways of men, the child changes his manner. Life will teach him when to stay firm in his thoughts and when to be pliable. If he has been guided correctly in his youth, it does not matter which way these thoughts go. It is still the Way. In time, some will learn to yield to strength more apparent than their own and they will prosper. Others will not. It is easy to cut down a mighty oak, but very difficult to cut down bamboo.

Because all things change, there is no way to hold onto anything in only one manner. Resiliency is the key and even in old age there is the possibility that brittle bones will be able to withstand the pressures of destruction. Ascension to Heaven is revealed.

Why is this wisdom so simple? Why is it so hard to understand? It is neither. It is the Way.

77

Heaven yields to man's desires
Man thinks he is in control
Failing to realize the pleasures
God enjoys by giving

Jealousy of God's power is foolish
It is the nature of man himself
As a bow stretched taut and ready to fire God's will stands
And flexing with looseness and congeniality
It looses the arrow into the target
With ease on either end
A man should understand his gifts

If he is given too much he will always want for more
If he is given not enough he will always want for more
The wise man always has enough
His abundance is ever increasing
Until his own wisdom shouts "Enough"

Heaven will abide fools as well as wise men, not caring to distinguish between the two. Heaven exalts what desires to be exalted. Heaven is impersonal and does not care for either desire. God does not strike down the evil and does not raise up the virtuous. Man does that by his own thinking. How could it be otherwise if the earth is filled with man's desires? That God is all good is acceptance of the virtue of the ever-expanding universe. Some things are unexplainable. Some things are unknowable. God is not one of them. God simply is.

Ever-increasing abundance is a gift that man must learn to accept as his divine birthright. Heaven does not create to destroy. If it did, it would also destroy itself because there would be no need for it to exist. The wise man knows that, for the universe to continue to expand and grow in all directions including the eight unknown, there must be a continual desire for all things to grow as well. That is why there is always an increase in population and an increase in heavenly and earthly prosperity according to those who desire it.

When a man dies he does not cease to exist on the universal level. The soul returns to Heaven and there its energy is revitalized into something else. This something else is not knowable to man because man cannot know what Heaven is. Even if man were to transcend death as he knows it and was able to return to his finite condition here on earth, he still would not know the ultimate reason for the universe. That is God's business and God's business alone.

78

Water as weakness
That is its strength
Pliable it constantly yields to form
The mightiest mountain falls prey to it
Desire diverts it from its path

All things in other forms prevail
Strength subsides because it is rigid
Pliable it is irresistible

So like water strong and weak
Is man's spirit strong and weak

Only one who can understand this can understand
Paradox as its own virtue

There is no such thing as one Way. It is therefore all things. There could not be one Way as differentiated from another unless man were strong enough to recognize his being as true strength leading to absolute power.

Which it is. The wise king understands that, to rule, it is essential to know all the needs of the people more than his own. Only by taking the responsibility of command and adoring its hideous weight can he rule with understanding and wisdom. By yielding to the people, his strength shows. By being pliable, he remains firm and in place.

The universe as all things must be all things. If it were not, it would have its own idea of totality. Not needing man to direct the cosmic energy would be the shortcoming of God because then man could know no pleasure. The all is all, though only a part of it. What a man knows indicates to him that he also knows that which is unknown.

79

Arguments settled one-sidedly

One party will feel disadvantaged

The other will think they are righteous

Judges end up fools

Assuaging both parties

Virtue takes dominance

In a man's mind

It is best to reach mutual accord

Which is easily done

If no man is held to blame

Reason not rhyme

The role of judge is difficult but reason, not legality, should pave the way for justice. Proving one man wrong and another right leaves anger in the heart of one and fear in the heart of the other. Of what value is the judge if he cannot bring peace to all parties regardless of each side's arguments? Thus he takes into consideration the commission of the deed as well.

It is not wise to permit legality to rule the day when justice can maintain peace and harmony throughout the land. No one is beyond recrimination. Foul deeds will only breed more foul deeds. A man who wishes to be judge must first cleanse his own heart and live in the Way. Then he will not wish to judge and all will be harmonious. Then he will be sought out and, if he is truly wise, will know the importance of understanding his own self in relation to the matter being judged. To judge correctly, have no friends. Then all men will befriend you.

80

A land is filled with peace
People are filled with work
Tools abound boats and carts
Their labors are a joy

Weapons are there
Armor as well
Stores remain on hand
Unused unseen unnecessary

Counters are correct
Food is plentiful
Children smile
Old people sit in the sun
Fed by the strong
All is well

 In this utopian atmosphere, all seems to be perfect and
all seems to be in the mind of the Way. And so it is, but
the reality of the world is such that the people are pre-

pared for any eventuality that the Heavens may visit upon them. This is true wisdom. It is not living in a state of purported bliss. That can never be in the finite. In time, neighboring lands may feel that they are treated unjustly and will take their revenge against the utopian condition. They will be surprised because all that is necessary for survival is already in place and out of sight of the invaders who will thirst and go hungry should they try to invade. The people will continue on their Way. "Counters are correct" means that those in charge of ensuring tranquillity will see that no false counts are recorded.

Being aware of your surroundings gives you the advantage of living in harmony while knowing that others about you may not be content with their lots in life. Constantly trying to improve themselves at the expense of those in the Way of harmony is to be expected. It must also be known that those of weakness will always try to weaken those of strength. It is their Way. It does not mean that you should permit this to happen. Maintain your own strength by examples of being just. Do not permit misunderstood sympathy to lead you to empathy. Never let the weak try to become strong through you. It cannot be done and will only weaken you, bringing you down to their level. They must ascend to their own levels.

If men are not strong, it is because they think they are not in the Way of Heaven. They are not correct and should endeavor to make a place in Heaven for themselves. Then they will not need to usurp the strength of the strong.

81

Reality is not vain nor are the words that bring it

Clever verse is not based on knowing

The good do not argue

Arguers are not good

Knowers are not the learned in the land

The learned in the land are not the knowers

Wise men do not hoard their possessions

They rid themselves of the weight

But thus giving all to all

They have more than they can ever use

Heaven seeks no gain

Wise men do their work

When they leave they cannot get away

What folly it is to have things that can only weigh you down with their apparent value. It is better to permit Heaven to give you all that you need, for all that you need. There is no reason for man to seek profit and gain. It is only something that he will lose in time.

Seek victory by living in harmony with yourself. Accept all that is and enjoy your devotion to the Way.

That is the Way.

Other books by Stephen F. Kaufman, Hanshi 10th Dan

The Art of War
The Definitive Interpretation of Sun Tzu's Classic
Book of Strategy for the Martial Artist

Sun Tzu's Art of War is perhaps the best-known treatise on strategy yet written and this definitive edition is by and for martial artists. It is a no-holds-barred interpretation, free of academic commentary and ambiguous metaphors.

136 pages 0-8048-3080-0 paperback

The Martial Artist's Book of Five Rings
The Definitive Interpretation of Miyamoto Musashi's
Classic Book of Strategy

Here is an interpretation of The Book of Five Rings, the ancient text on the samurai code, written specifically for the martial artist. This is Hanshi Kaufman's best-selling book.

128 pages 0-8048-3020-7 paperback

The Shogun Scrolls
On Controlling All Aspects of the Realm

The Shogun Scrolls were written in the twelfth century by Hidetomo Nakadai, the first shogun of Japan. They are interpreted here and can be used today as a guide for personal development and motivation.

128 pages 0-8048-3122- X paperback

For a complete catalog of martial arts
and philosophy books call or write to:

Tuttle Publishing
RR1 Box 231-5
North Clarendon, VT   05759-9700
phone: (802) 773-8930
fax: (802) 773-6993
toll-free: (800) 526-2778